FAT QUARTER
VINTAGE

25 projects to make from short lengths of fabric

Susie Johns

THE GUILD OF MASTER CRAFTSMAN PUBLICATIONS

First published 2019 by
Guild of Master Craftsman Publications Ltd
Castle Place, 166 High Street, Lewes,
East Sussex, BN7 1XU, UK

Text © Susie Johns, 2019
Copyright in the Work © GMC Publications Ltd, 2019

ISBN 978 1 78494 421 6

A catalogue record for this book is available from the British Library.

Publisher Jonathan Bailey
Production Jim Bulley and Jo Pallett
Senior Project Editor Dominique Page
Editor Sarah Hoggett
Managing Art Editor Gilda Pacitti
Design & Art Direction Wayne Blades
Photographer Neal Grundy
Step photography Susie Johns

Colour origination by GMC Reprographics

Printed and bound in China

A note on measurements
The imperial measurements in these projects are converted from metric. While every attempt has been made to ensure that they are as accurate as possible, some rounding up or down has been inevitable. For this reason, it is always best to stick to one system or the other throughout a project: do not mix metric and imperial units.

CONTENTS

INTRODUCTION

If you're anything like me, you will find it hard to resist buying lovely fabrics when you see them in shops, fairs and markets, even when you don't have a project in mind. Added to bits left over from sewing sessions, you end up with a stash of offcuts and remnants. The colours and patterns of vintage fabrics evoke the period when they were made. Genuine vintage fabrics are becoming harder to source, but some manufacturers offer reprints or new designs with a retro feel.

These days we tend to sew from choice, but for past generations it was often from necessity. In the Depression of the 1930s, many people found they had to mend clothes and make do with less. At the same time, the Arts and Crafts movement, which began in the late 1900s, was still influential and inspired people to be creative. During World War Two, austerity continued. Women were encouraged to sew for the war effort and to attend classes at college to learn how to 'make do and mend' – what we call 'upcycling' nowadays. In the post-war boom of the 1950s, people could afford to buy clothes and soft furnishings but sewing was still popular, with many people copying styles from the pages of glossy magazines. With the youth movement of the 1960s, younger women developed a passion for sewing. Then, in the 1970s, with hippy chic handcrafts, sewing enthusiasts customized and altered clothes, and enjoyed patchwork and appliqué.

To make your own projects with a retro feel, fat quarters are a good way to build up a collection of fabrics. What is a fat quarter? It's a way of cutting a yard or metre of fabric into four to create pieces approximately 18 x 22in (46 x 56cm). This squarish shape is, for most projects, far more versatile; buying fat quarters also makes it possible to buy four different fabrics for the same cost as a yard or metre of a single design.

The 25 practical and stylish projects in this book will help you to make the most of your fat quarters: the makes are suitable for medium-weight cotton or linen fabrics. Choose your favourite decade – the 1930s, 40s, 50s, 60s or 70s – and personalize your item by choosing your own combinations of colours and patterns, then create something that evokes the style of days gone by.

Susie

THE BASICS

MATERIALS & EQUIPMENT

If you are keen on sewing, you will no doubt have most of the tools and equipment needed to complete the projects in this book. All you will have to buy are some fat quarters of fabrics in your choice of colours and designs.

MEASURING Use either metric or imperial measurements: both are included in the pattern instructions, but do not mix the two.

You will need a long ruler for drawing lines on fabric, as well as a tape measure. A set square, right-angled ruler or quilter's square helps to measure and mark out neat corners. Other useful measuring devices are available, such as gauges for marking evenly spaced lines and for helping to ensure neatly turned hems.

SCISSORS You will need dressmaking scissors for cutting fabrics and small, pointed embroidery scissors for snipping threads. Pinking shears are also useful for trimming raw edges on seams, to prevent fraying; they can also be used for cutting decorative shapes from felt. Use a separate pair of scissors for cutting paper, as paper tends to blunt the blades.

SEAM RIPPER This tool is useful for cutting individual stitches and unpicking seams without damaging the fabric. Insert the pointed blade underneath the stitch to be cut, then push it forwards against the thread.

PINS Before stitching, it is advisable to pin and tack (baste) layers of fabric together to prevent them from slipping when stitching. Pins with glass heads are easy to handle and to find. Sometimes, however, pins distort the fabric or are difficult to use when there are lots of layers or tough fabrics, in which case you may find it easier to use binding clips. Safety pins can be used in place of straight pins to hold fabric layers together; they are also useful for threading elastic and cords through casings.

NEEDLES Sharps are an all-rounder for hand sewing, with a round eye that is easy to thread. For embroidery, an embroidery needle has a longer eye, to accommodate thicker thread.

THREADS Use cotton thread when sewing cotton fabrics. It is available in a wide range of colours. Choose a thread to match the fabric as closely as possible, choosing a shade darker if you cannot find an exact match. For quilting and gathering, you can choose to use a slightly stronger thread, while for decorative stitching, embroidery thread (floss) is more substantial than ordinary sewing thread. Available in an enormous range of colours, the embroidery thread used in this book is six-stranded thread; this means that a single thick strand is made up from six thin strands twisted together. If you are directed to use two strands, for example, cut a length of thread from the skein and pull out two individual strands, then place the ends of these strands together and thread them through the eye of your embroidery needle.

EMBROIDERY HOOP For most types of embroidery, it is best to place the fabric to be stitched in an embroidery hoop, which holds it taut while you sew.

BOBBINS Keep a small stock of sewing-machine bobbins loaded with different coloured threads, ready for use. When combining different coloured fabrics, it can be useful to use one colour as a top thread and another on the bobbin.

IRON A good steam iron is an essential piece of equipment. Make sure that your ironing board is firm and stable, with a well-padded surface. Press fabrics before measuring and cutting, then press the work regularly when sewing, for a neat finish. When pressing embroidery, place the work right side down on a folded towel and press on the reverse; the towel cushions the fabric and helps to prevent the embroidery stitches from being flattened.

FABRICS Cotton and linen fabrics, both modern and vintage, are widely available as pre-cut fat quarters. These have been used throughout the book as the main fabrics. When searching for period fabrics, you will invariably come across 'barkcloth', which was a popular fabric for home furnishings throughout the 1930s, 40s and 50s; the term refers to the bark-like texture of the weave, rather than the fibre content. Where felt is used, make sure it is washable. Craft felt will fall apart when it is washed, so buy felt made from wool or a wool blend, and ask when buying if it can be laundered. If you are unsure, wash a sample in the washing machine before using it in a project.

TECHNIQUES

The majority of the projects in this book involve basic sewing techniques, both by hand and machine. In this section you will find some basic instructions and tips to help you achieve a neat and professional-looking result.

PREPARING TO SEW

Preparation is important when embarking on any new project – and before you start sewing, there are a number of things you will need to do first.

MARKING FABRIC

When a project is made up of squares, rectangles and strips of fabric, measurements are given within the pattern instructions. You will need to measure and mark out these shapes on your fabric, using a ruler or a set square. More complex pattern pieces are printed at the back of the book, as templates. These need to be traced; or if they need to be enlarged, you can photocopy them. Larger pattern pieces, to be pinned to the fabric, can be cut from paper – such as brown parcel paper, or dressmaker's paper printed with a helpful grid. Smaller templates, especially those that you need to draw around, can be cut from card. Instead of card, especially for pieces that you will want to draw around again and again, you will find that plastic is more robust and you can buy semi-transparent sheets sold especially for this purpose; once again, this material is available printed with a grid, which you might find helpful.

For drawing on fabric, use tailor's chalk or a chalk pencil, which can be rubbed away afterwards. Alternatively, you could use a water-erasable marker pen. An ordinary pencil or ballpoint pen can be used where the marks will be hidden in the seams or on the inside of the finished item, and also for drawing out designs to be embroidered when the lines will be completely hidden by the stitches.

When transferring the motifs for embroidery on to fabric, the easiest method is to trace them directly on to the fabric. To do this, you may first need to trace or photocopy each one onto plain paper, then use a light box so that you can clearly see the outline to be traced. If you don't have a light box, try taping the paper to a window and taping the fabric on top.

INTERFACING AND WADDING (BATTING)

To add substance and sometimes stiffness to cotton fabrics, other materials are applied to the fabric pieces before they are assembled. The type and weight you need will be specified in the project. Fusible interfacing is a non-woven material that stiffens the fabric; it is available in three weights: light, medium and heavy. Fusible fleece is a soft, felted fabric that adds a little thickness and softness. Wadding (batting) – used in quilt making – also creates extra padding.

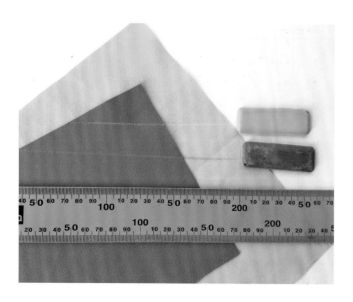

When using fusible materials, first identify which side of the material is adhesive and place it face down on the wrong side of the fabric. Place a piece of non-stick baking parchment on top, to protect the base plate of the iron. You may also wish to place some scrap fabric between the fabric and the surface of the ironing board. The heat from the iron will melt the adhesive and bond the interfacing or other material to the fabric. Try not to glide the iron, as this may cause the layers of fabric and interfacing to shift.

HAND SEWING

Sometimes it is necessary to sew by hand, with a needle and thread, either prior to, or instead of, machine sewing.

TACKING (BASTING)

Tacking is used to join layers of fabric together prior to sewing. Use a long running stitch for tacking. Start and finish with a couple of stitches worked over each other to secure the end of the thread, and work the stitches within the seam allowance.

SLIPSTITCH

When making items such as cushion covers or objects to be stuffed, you will need to join pieces with right sides together, leaving a gap for turning that then has to be closed on the right side. Use slipstitch for this, for a neat and barely visible result. Fold in the raw edges on each side of the gap, then secure the thread in the end of the seam. Use the tip of the needle to pick up a small section of fabric along the fold on one side. Then pick up a small amount of fabric on the other side. Pull the thread to close the gap. Repeat all along the opening and fasten off.

EMBROIDERY

Embroidery was a popular craft during all the decades covered by this book. It is different from other types of sewing, in that it is not used to hold two pieces of fabric together but to provide decoration. It is a lovely way to show your creativity and, even if you are new to embroidery, it is quite easy to achieve good results.

CHAIN STITCH

This looped stitch can be worked along a curved or straight line. It can also be worked as an individual stitch, perfect for representing a small leaf; here it is called 'detached chain stitch'.

Bring the needle up through the fabric at the starting point. Insert the needle again in the same place, then bring the tip up through the fabric a short distance away. Loop the working thread around the tip of the needle and pull it through the loop. For a row of chain stitches (top), re-insert the needle in the same place, just inside the loop, and repeat the process to make a line of linked stitches that form a chain. At the end of the line, make a small, straight stitch to anchor the final loop in place.

For a detached chain stitch or 'lazy daisy' (bottom left), simply reinsert the needle through the fabric on the other side of this loop, so that it is held in place with a tiny stitch– just like the final anchoring stitch in a row of chain stitches.

BLANKET STITCH

Blanket stitch is used to edge blankets; it can also be used to attach appliqué shapes to a background fabric. Buttonhole stitch is the same, the difference being that stitches are worked close together.

Push the needle up through the fabric at the edge of the appliqué shape and bring it back out directly below, through the background fabric and the appliqué. This creates a small loop at the top. Take the needle up through the loop and pull to tighten the stitch; the vertical thread is now held in place by a small horizontal bar that runs along the edge of the appliqué shape. You can choose the height of the stitch as you insert the needle and you can also alter the space between stitches.

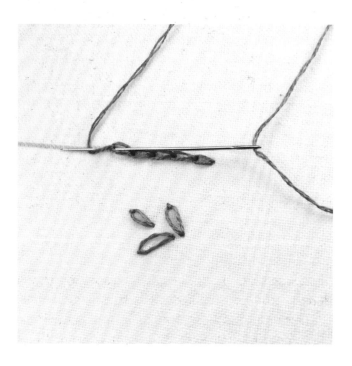

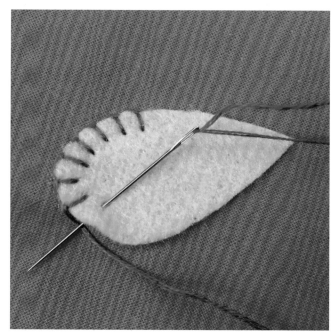

SATIN STITCH

This is suitable for filling small areas of a design. Work straight, parallel stitches closely together to cover the shape to be filled. There should be no gaps between the stitches. Try to keep the fabric smooth and taut to ensure that all your stitches lie flat.

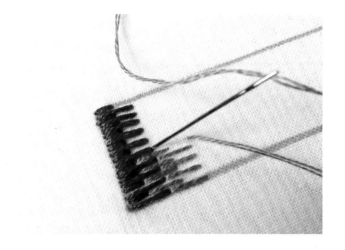

Long and short stitch is a variation used when there are larger shapes to be filled. It can be worked in a single colour, or each row can be worked in a different colour or in different shades of the same colour, for a variegated effect. Work the first row in alternating long and short stitches and the second and subsequent rows in stitches that are the same length as each other, taking the needle into the fabric at the end of the corresponding stitch on the previous rows, so that alternate stitches end up being offset, or 'stepped'.

BACKSTITCH

This stitch is particularly useful for outlining; it is also essential for stitching strong seams by hand.

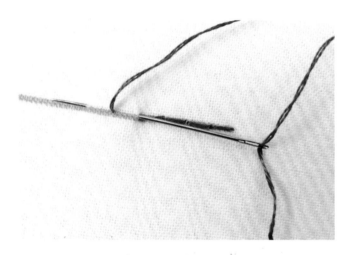

Thread the needle with the desired number of strands of thread: embroidery thread for decorative work and sewing thread for hand-sewn seams. Working from right to left, bring the needle up through the fabric a stitch length along the line or outline, then back down through the fabric at the beginning of the line. Bring the needle up again a stitch length along from the first stitch; repeat the process, going back in again at the starting point of that stitch, then forward a stitch length in front.

SPLIT STITCH

This stitch is useful for outlining, embroidering lines and filling larger shapes.

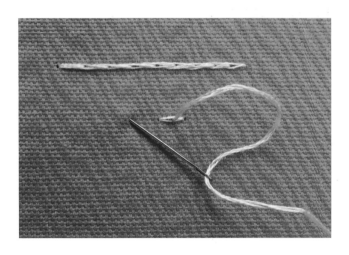

Thread the needle with the desired number of strands of embroidery thread. Bring the needle up through the fabric at the beginning of the line or outline, then down a little way along. Bring the needle up through the centre of the stitch you just made. Take the needle back down through the fabric a little way along; keep the stitches reasonably short. Repeat the process along the length of the line. For thicker lines, or to fill shapes, work a second or further rows of split stitches parallel to the first.

STEM STITCH

This stitch is, as its name suggests, particularly useful for embroidering stems, but also for any line or outline.

Working from left to right, bring the needle up at the beginning of the line to be worked, then down a stitch length to the right, just below the line or outline. Pull the thread through to form the first stitch, then bring the tip of the needle up through the fabric just above the centre of the first stitch, then along the line to the right once more. Repeat this process.

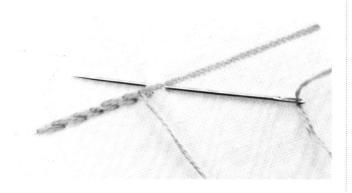

FRENCH KNOTS

Bring the needle through to the right side of the fabric. Hold the thread close to the surface of the fabric and wrap it around the needle three times. Pull the thread tight and re-insert the needle close to where it emerged. Keeping the tension on the wrapped thread, pull the needle through to the back of the work; the knot that is formed should sit on the surface of the fabric.

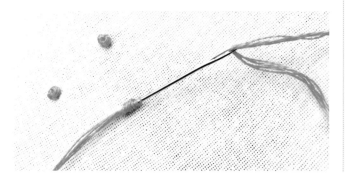

MACHINE SEWING

Most of the projects in this book are made using a sewing machine and straight-stitch seams, to ensure that components are firmly joined together. Use the right size needle for the fabric – size 80 for medium-weight cotton – and change it frequently to ensure that the needle is sharp.

SETTING UP

Place the machine where there is plenty of light and you can sit comfortably. Make sure that the machine is threaded correctly and that the threads from the needle and the bobbin are placed away from you, towards the back of the base plate. When you start to stitch, turn the hand wheel to lower the needle into the fabric; this will help to prevent the threads from tangling. Before stitching your project, test the machine-stitch size and tension on a scrap of the fabric you are working with, and adjust if necessary.

STRAIGHT STITCH

This is used for flat seams and topstitching, and for hemming. You can alter the length of the stitch, using a long stitch for basting and gathering, for example. At the start and end of a line of stitching, backstitch for a few stitches. This will prevent the stitches from coming undone and you can snip off the threads close to the surface of the fabric.

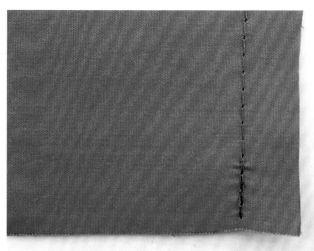

TOPSTITCHING

Topstitching creates a crisp finish and an element of decoration – and also holds layers of fabric neatly and securely in place. Press the seam to one side. Topstitch parallel to the seamline; the distance from the line is variable, but on a seam it will be a smaller measurement than the seam allowance to ensure that the raw edges of the fabric are trapped under the topstitching.

ZIGZAG STITCH

Zigzag stitch is decorative and practical. It can be used to attach appliqué shapes (see Appliqué Cushion, pages 90–93). It is also useful for neatening raw edges on seams, to prevent fraying.

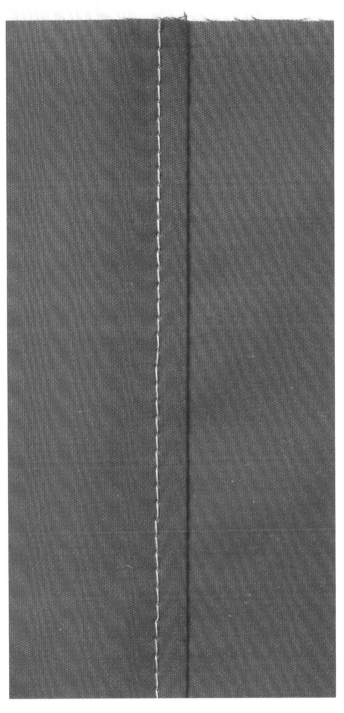

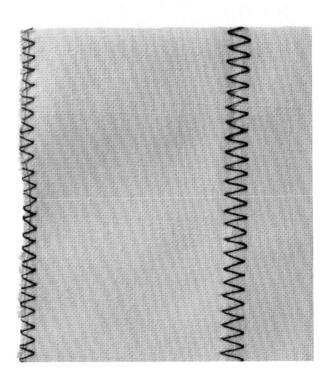

ADDITIONAL TECHNIQUES

Throughout the book, you will come across certain methods to help you achieve a neat result. If you are a seasoned stitcher, these may already be familiar to you but you may also find some helpful hints and tips on these pages.

BINDING EDGES

Bias binding is a great way to finish an edge on all kinds of items. Bias binding is inexpensive and available in a wide range of colours, plain and printed, and in several widths. Here are two different techniques for applying it.

ONE-STEP BINDING

This method works best on a straight edge of firm fabric. Fold the binding in half down its length and press. Place the folded binding over the edge of the fabric, to enclose it completely. Pin and tack in place, then stitch close to the lower edge of the binding, checking on the other side that the stitching has captured both long edges.

TWO-STEP BINDING

When binding an uneven edge, a corner or curve, two-step binding is the preferred method.

1 Open out the binding and line up one raw edge of the binding with the edge of the fabric. Pin and tack to hold in place, then stitch along the fold line by hand or machine.

2 Fold the binding over to enclose the raw edges, and slipstitch the other long folded edge of the binding on the stitch line.

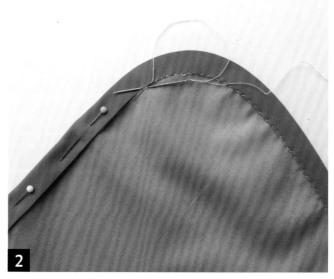

USING A CORNER AND EDGE SHAPER

When items or components need to be turned right sides out, it is often necessary to use a tool to push out the corners neatly without displacing the stitches or tearing the fabric. A blunt object such as a knitting needle can be used for this; however, you may want to consider investing in a purpose-made corner and edge shaper, which is a flat, blade-shaped object with a pointed end for sharp corners, a curved end for rounded shapes (such as the dog's ears on the draught excluder, page 112), and straight edges for pushing out seams before pressing.

CLIPPING CORNERS AND CURVES

Corners should be cut across at an angle so that they are sharp when the work is turned right side out. On curved seams, cut 'V' shapes into the seam allowance, close to the stitch line. Snip very carefully to avoid cutting through the stitches by mistake.

USING A LOOP TURNER

Making a narrow tube of fabric can be fiddly, but the task is easier if you use a loop turner – a long metal pin with a ring on one end and a clip on the other. Insert the loop turner into the tube of fabric and attach the clip to the end of the seam, then pull the loop turner back through the tube.

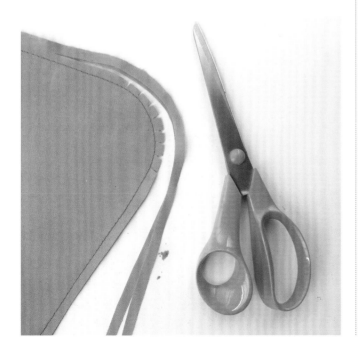

1930s

NEEDLE CASE

Between the wars, during the 1920s and 30s, magazines provided women with a multitude of ideas for sewing and other crafts, and embroidery was in its heyday. Celebrate this golden age of creativity with a needle case for yourself or to give as a gift.

You will need
Printed cotton fabric,
    at least 8 x 6in (20 x 15cm)
Plain cotton fabric, for lining,
    at least 8 x 6in (20 x 15cm)
Medium-weight fusible interfacing,
    at least 8 x 6in (20 x 15cm)
Fusible fleece, at least 8 x 6in (20 x 15cm)
Vintage embroidered coaster,
    no larger than 5in (13cm) in diameter
Felt, at least 14 x 6in (36 x 15cm)
10in (25cm) length of narrow ribbon
Pencil or fabric marker
Dressmaking scissors
Pinking shears
Pins
Sewing machine
Sewing needle
Thread for tacking (basting)
Thread to match fabric
Iron and ironing board
Non-stick baking parchment
Corner and edge shaper (see page 21)
    or similar tool, such as a knitting needle

Finished size is roughly:
7¼ x 5¼in (18.5 x 13.5cm)

NOTE: Antique linens like the little embroidered coaster used to decorate this needle case are widely available from markets and charity shops. No longer used on a daily basis, table linens can be re-purposed in all kinds of sewing projects – such as the coat hanger cover on page 54.

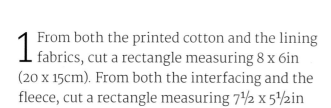
1 From both the printed cotton and the lining fabrics, cut a rectangle measuring 8 x 6in (20 x 15cm). From both the interfacing and the fleece, cut a rectangle measuring 7½ x 5½in (19 x 14cm).

2 Centre the interfacing on the wrong side of the lining fabric and the fleece on the wrong side of the printed cotton. Place a piece of non-stick baking parchment on top of the fusible fabrics to protect the base plate of the iron. Following the manufacturer's instructions and using a hot iron, fuse the fabrics together (see page 15).

3 Centre the little coaster right side up on the right side of the printed cotton fabric. Pin it in place, then slipstitch all around (see page 15) to attach it to the fabric.

4 Cut the ribbon in half to make two 5in (12.5cm) lengths. Pin one end of each ribbon to a short edge of the printed cotton fabric; tack (baste) in place.

5 Place the main and lining fabrics, right sides together, aligning the edges; pin and tack. Mark a gap on one long edge by placing pins approximately 3in (8cm) apart.

6 Machine stitch all round with a $^3/_8$in (1cm) seam allowance, leaving the gap between the pins unstitched. Snip off the corners.

7 Turn the needle case right side out and push out the corners using a corner and edge shaper or similar tool.

8 Turn the seam allowance to the inside along the edges of the gap, then press.

9 Slipstitch the folded edges securely together to close the gap.

10 On the felt mark out two rectangles, each measuring 7$^1/_8$ x 5$^1/_8$in (18 x 13cm). Cut out using pinking shears.

11 Fold each piece of felt in half and press. Fold the cover in half and press, then open it out.

12 Pin the felt pieces to the inside of the needle case, matching the centres, and stitch along the fold, through all layers, by hand with a neat running stitch.

Tip

Modern craft felt is made from acrylic, so if you want to be authentic, you may prefer to use a wool felt for the 'pages' of this little needle book.

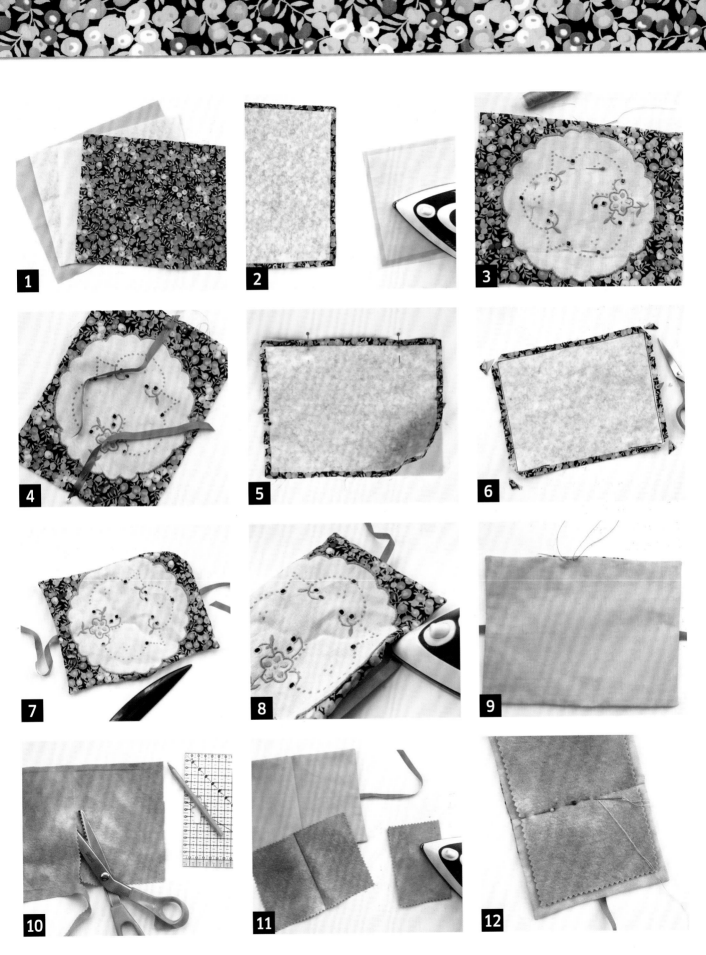

PINCUSHION

Turn a teacup into a pretty pincushion. Odd cups can be picked up cheaply at antique fairs and markets and this little gem requires only the minimum of sewing. It would make a lovely gift, especially with a co-ordinating mini pincushion in an egg cup.

You will need
Printed fabric, approximately 9½in (24cm) square
Tights
China teacup
Drinking glass or jam jar
Crushed walnut shells, approximately 7oz (200g)
Chalk pencil or fabric marker
Pins
Dressmaking scissors
General-purpose scissors
Sewing needle
Strong sewing thread
Iron and ironing board
Hot glue gun

Tip
You could choose to stuff your pincushion with wadding or a material of your choice, but crushed walnut shells are a traditional filling for pincushions, adding weight and also helping to sharpen the pins as you push them in.

1 Cut off one of the legs from the tights about 8in (20cm) from the toe. (You can discard the rest of the tights or save them to make more pincushions at another time.)

2 Stretch the piece you have cut from the tights over a container such as a drinking glass or jam jar. Using the teacup as a measure, pour about 7oz (200g) of crushed walnut shells into the foot of the tights.

3 Remove the foot of the tights from the glass, stretch this slightly and knot the end tightly. Cut off the excess.

4 Find a plate or similar round object about 8in (20cm) in diameter to use as a template. Draw around it with a chalk pencil on the wrong side of the fabric and cut out.

5 Thread a needle with a 10in (25cm) length of strong thread. Stitch a running stitch around the circle, about $^3/_{16}$in (4mm) from the edge.

6 Place the bag of walnut shells on the wrong side of the circle, in the centre, and pull up the thread ends to gather the fabric tightly. Knot the ends of the thread together securely, then cut off the excess thread.

7 Place the fabric-covered ball in the teacup to make sure it fits. You may need to manipulate it slightly, by squeezing it in your hands, to adjust the shape and make sure it fits snugly.

8 Apply a line of hot glue around the inside of the cup, about $^3/_4$in (2cm) below the rim. Immediately push the ball inside, before the glue has time to set.

Tip

To make a smaller version of the pincushion, use an egg cup. Follow the instructions for the cup, but cut a circle of fabric 4$^3/_4$in (12cm) in diameter.

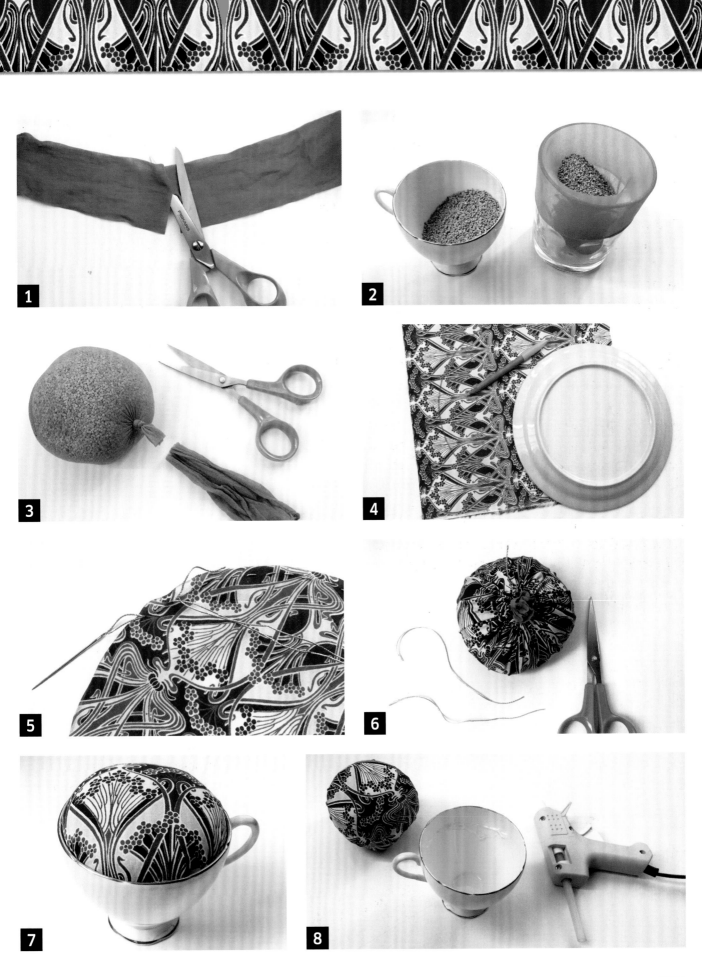

TRAY CLOTH

In the elegant 1930s, a lady's beauty routine involved sitting at her dressing table, brushing her hair, manicuring her nails and doing her make-up. A hairbrush, hand mirror and other accessories would be laid out, ready for use, on a decorative mat such as this one.

Find the templates on page 132

You will need
1 fat quarter of printed cotton fabric
1 fat quarter of plain cotton or linen fabric, for backing
White linen fabric, at least 11 x 8in (28 x 20cm)
DMC six-stranded embroidery threads (flosses):
   336 (indigo), 3347 (sage green) and 970 (orange)
40in (1m) of narrow satin ribbon
60in (1.5m) of ½in (12mm) bias binding
Pencil or erasable marking pen
Paper for making pattern
Pins
Dressmaking scissors
Embroidery scissors
General-purpose scissors
10in (25cm) embroidery hoop
Sewing machine
Embroidery needle
Sewing needle
Thread for tacking (basting)
Thread to match fabric
Iron and ironing board

Tip

You can use an erasable marking pen for marking the embroidery motif on the fabric; this means the lines can be erased after you've completed the embroidery (see page 14). Alternatively, use an ordinary pencil: this cannot be erased, but any pencil lines will be covered by the lines of chain stitch.

Finished size is roughly:
14 x 10¾in (35 x 27cm)

1 Using the template on page 132, make a paper pattern for the cloth (see page 14). Place the printed and plain fabrics together and pin the pattern in place; cut out the fabrics and reserve.

2 Mark out a rectangle measuring 10¼ x 7in (26 x 18cm) on white linen. Do not cut it out at this stage.

3 Trace the embroidery template on page 132 onto the linen (see page 14), placing it in opposite corners of the rectangle, about 1¼in (3cm) in from the line you have drawn.

4 Place the linen in an embroidery hoop. Cut a length of indigo embroidery thread (floss) and separate out three strands; thread these into an embroidery needle and begin by stitching the outlines of the stems and leaves in chain stitch (see page 16).

5 Again using three strands of thread and chain stitch, outline the small circle in jade green and the large circle in orange.

6 Cut out the embroidered rectangle along the lines you marked in step 2. Press it on the wrong side, using a hot iron.

7 Centre the embroidered rectangle right side up on the right side of the patterned fabric; pin and tack (baste) it in place.

8 Stitch the embroidered panel in place all around, by hand or by machine, stitching close to the raw edge. Cover the raw edge with ribbon, slipstitching the edges of the ribbon to the fabric (see page 15). On each corner, fold the ribbon to create a neat mitre (see page 20).

9 Place the patterned fabric on top of the backing fabric, wrong sides together. Pin and tack together, close to the edges.

10 Bind the raw edges with bias binding, using the two-step method described on page 20.

Tip

The two-step binding method used to edge the tray cloth is the best way to bind a curved or wavy edge. Because it requires hand sewing, it may take a little more time but the finished result will be very neat.

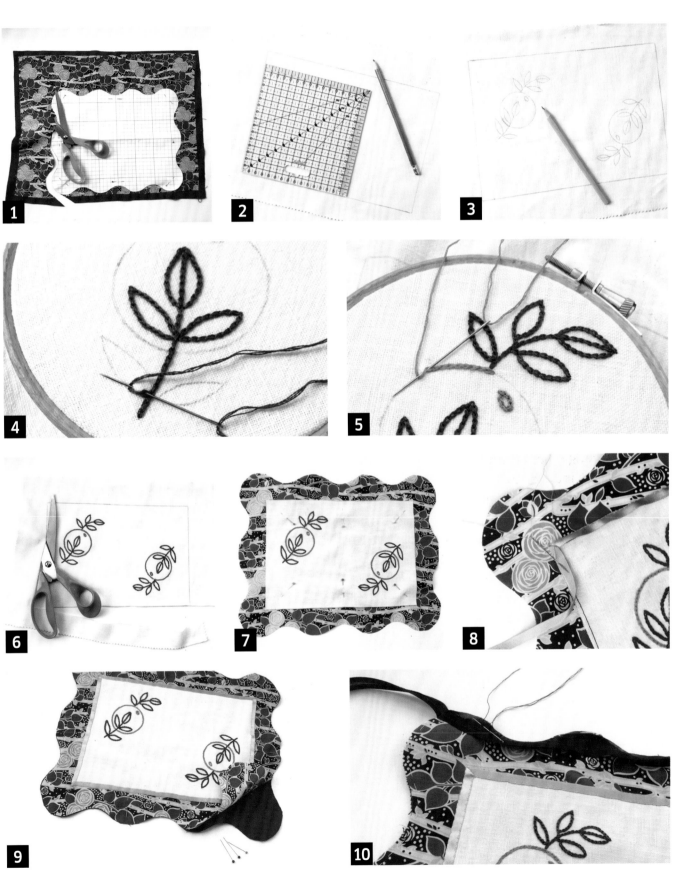

EMBROIDERED CUSHION

The crinoline lady was popular throughout the 1930s, decorating tray cloths, tea cosies and tablecloths, as well as cushions like this one. Choose a suitable print for the back of the cushion and the front border: the fabric used here is a classic print from Liberty of London.

Find the template on page 133

Tip

You can choose your own palette of embroidery threads or use the ones suggested here. Use the picture of the finished embroidery as a guide to colour placement and the various stitches used. You will find detailed instructions for the stitches on pages 15–19.

You will need
1 fat quarter of white cotton or linen fabric
2 fat quarters of printed fabric
DMC six-stranded embroidery thread in the following colours:
    640 (khaki), 3346 (olive green), 704 (grass green), 436 (tan),
    3722 (dusky pink), 352 (salmon pink), 754 (pale peach),
    3846 (turquoise blue), 826 (saxe blue), 340 (lavender), 742 (yellow)
16in (40cm) square cushion pad
Pen or pencil, or tailor's chalk
Water-erasable marking pen
10in (25cm) embroidery hoop
Pins
Dressmaking scissors
General-purpose scissors
Sewing machine
Embroidery needle
Thread for tacking (basting)
Thread to match fabric
Iron and ironing board

NOTE: The stitches used to embroider crinoline lady designs were simple, with outlines in stem stitch, satin stitch filling, and plenty of French knots and detached chain stitches – also known as 'lazy daisy' – for the flowers.

Finished size is:
16in (40cm) square

1 Using a pen or pencil, or tailor's chalk, draw an 11in (28cm) square on the white fabric.

2 Using a pencil or a water-erasable marking pen, trace the motif on page 133 onto the centre of the fabric (see page 14).

3 Place the fabric in an embroidery hoop. Embroider the lines on the house and path in stem stitch, in khaki thread. Also in stem stitch, embroider all the flower stems in olive green.

NOTE: Use two strands of embroidery thread (floss) throughout.

4 Using two strands of grass green, embroider the leaves in detached chain stitch. Don't worry if the stitches don't cover up the drawn lines and shapes, as these will be erased later.

5 Embroider the flower petals in detached chain stitch, in lavender.

6 Embroider some of the flower shapes in dusky pink. Take the needle up through the outline of each circle and down through the centre, to produce radiating lines of satin stitch. Use salmon pink and lavender for the other flowers.

7 Fill in some of the larger shapes: fill in the door in satin stitch, using saxe blue, and use the same colour to outline the windows in stem stitch. Fill in the roof in long-and-short stitch, using yellow.

8 Using the same colours as in step 6, add French knots, indicated by tiny circles and dots. For the crinoline lady herself, use a combination of satin stitch, stem stitch, detached chain stitch and French knots, using the picture of the finished cushion – or your own imagination – as a guide for the colour.

9 If you marked out the pattern using a water-soluble pen, take the finished embroidery out of the hoop and immerse it in water to remove the drawn lines. Squeeze gently to remove excess water and leave to dry, then press on the reverse to remove any creases. Cut out the square panel.

10 From one fat quarter of printed fabric, cut two strips measuring $16^3/4$ x $3^1/2$in (42 x 9cm) and two at 11 x $3^1/2$in (28 x 9cm). Machine stitch the two smaller pieces to the top and bottom of the embroidered square with a $3/8$in (1cm) seam. Press the seams towards the border.

11 Machine stitch the two larger pieces to the side edges of the embroidered square and press the seams towards the borders. This now forms the cushion front. From the second fat quarter, cut a $16^3/4$in (42cm) square for the back. Place the two right sides together and machine stitch all round with a $3/8$in (1cm) seam allowance, leaving a gap of approximately 10in (25cm) on the lower edge. Snip off the corners.

12 Turn the cover right side out and press. Insert the cushion pad. Turn the seam allowance to the inside along the edges of the gap, then press. Slipstitch the folded edges securely together to close the gap (see page 15).

PYJAMA CASE

Both practical and pretty, this pyjama case is not only a useful place to tidy away your night clothes but also a decorative accessory for your bedroom. Show off your embroidery skills on a 1930s fabric, genuine or reproduction.

Find the template on page 134

You will need
2 fat quarters of white cotton fabric
1 fat quarter of printed cotton fabric
DMC six-stranded embroidery threads (flosses):
    977 (mustard), 351 (coral pink), 798 (cobalt), 797 (ultramarine)
Pencil or erasable fabric marker
Pins
Dressmaking scissors
Pinking shears
Embroidery scissors
Sewing machine
Sewing needle
Thread to match fabric
Iron and ironing board

Finished size is roughly:
10¼ x 11in (26 x 28 cm)

1 Trace the design from page 134 onto one half of one of the white fat quarters (see page 14), using a pencil or an erasable marker pen.

2 Using the appropriate colour of thread (floss), sew two lines of running stitch between the double lines of the design to stabilize the fabric and act as padding; refer to the photograph of the finished case for the placement of colours.

NOTE: Use two strands of thread throughout for the embroidery.

3 Using the running-stitch lines as a guide, embroider the design in buttonhole stitch. Start with the flower centres, using mustard thread, then embroider the outlines of the flowers, using coral pink. Then embroider the stems in dark blue and the leaves in a lighter shade of blue.

4 Embroider the leaf veins and the stamens of the flowers in backstitch (see page 17), using the appropriate colour.

5 Add a French knot (see page 18), using mustard thread, at the end of each stamen.

6 If you've used a water-soluble marker pen, immerse the fabric in water to remove the blue lines, then leave it to dry. Press on the wrong side. Measure and mark out a line on the wrong side, 1in (2.5cm) from the upper corners of the embroidered motif.

7 Cut along the line you have drawn, then pin the two pieces of fabric right sides together.

8 Using white thread, backstitch by hand all around the outer (shaped) edge of the embroidery, stitching through both layers and working the stitches as close as possible to the edge of the embroidery stitches. Extend the line of stitches up to the straight edge on either side. Using pinking shears, cut out about 1/4in (6mm) from the stitch line.

9 Turn the embroidered panel right side out and press it on the unembroidered side.

10 Measure and cut a rectangle 21 1/4 x 11 3/4 in (54 x 30cm) from both the second white fat quarter and the printed fat quarter. Fold each one in half lengthways, right sides together, and machine stitch the side seams with a 3/8in (1cm) seam allowance to make an outer bag and a lining.

11 Turn the outer bag right side out. Press both the outer bag and the lining. Along the raw top edges, fold 3/8in (1cm) to the wrong side and press.

12 Slip the lining inside the outer bag, matching the side seams and lining up the folded edges. Then fold the raw edge of the embroidered piece, which forms the flap, in between the main part and the lining on one side. Pin in place. On the back of the cover, slipstitch (see page 15) the edges of the main fabric and lining to the flap; on the front, slipstitch the folded edges of the bag and lining together.

Tip

The colours used here for the embroidery complement the pattern on the fabric, but you could choose different colours, to match the fabric you are using.

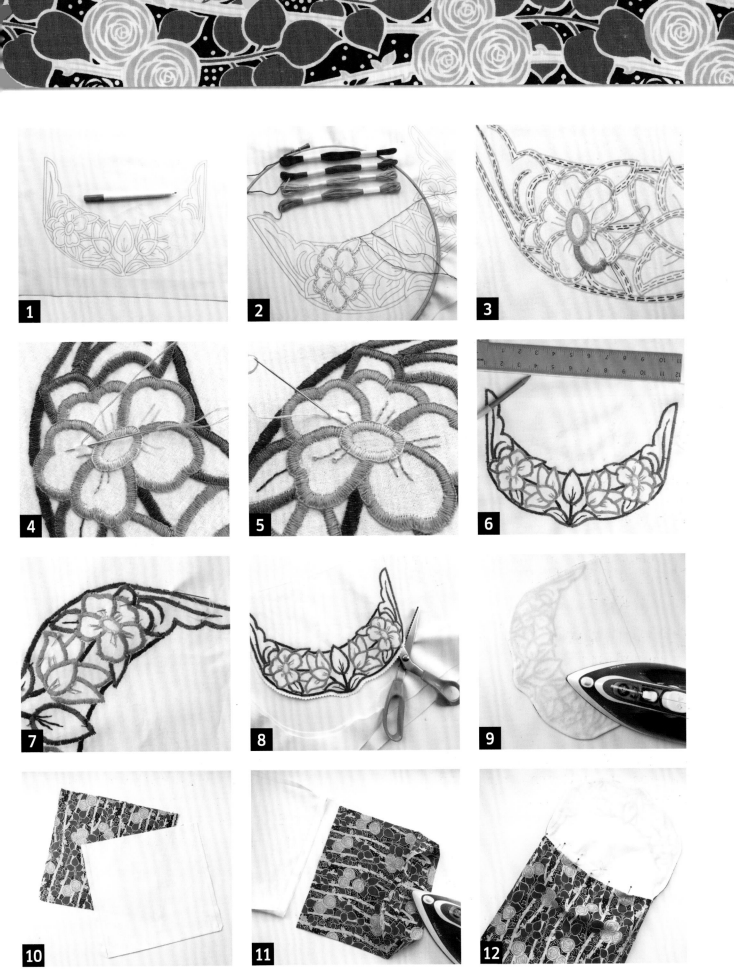

1940s

FLOWER BROOCH

This fabric flower brooch should appeal to anyone who enjoys wearing vintage clothing, providing a pretty finishing touch to any outfit. It would look lovely on the lapel of a jacket or coat, for example, or pinned to a hatband.

You will need
Vintage printed cotton or linen fabric,
    at least 12 x 10in (30 x 25cm)
Self-covering button, 1½in (4cm) in diameter
Small scrap of felt
Brooch pin
Pencil or fabric marker
Pins
Dressmaking scissors
Sewing needle
Strong thread
Thread to match fabric
Iron and ironing board

Tip
*Self-covering buttons vary.
If yours is different from the one
shown in these steps, follow the
manufacturer's instructions to
cover the button.*

Finished size is roughly:
4in (10cm) in diameter

1 Using an object such as a teacup, with a diameter of $3\frac{1}{8}$in (8cm), draw seven circles on the fabric. Cut them out. Set aside one of the circles: this will be used to cover the button that will form the centre of the flower.

2 Fold the six circles that will form the petals in half and then in half again to form a quarter circle; press.

3 Thread a needle with a length of strong thread. Place one of the quarter circles with its curved edge uppermost, fasten the thread to the right-hand corner and sew a running stitch around the curve through all thicknesses, leaving a long tail of thread at the start of the stitching.

4 Take a second quarter circle and continue the running stitch along this curved edge.

5 Repeat step 4 until you have joined all six petals together.

6 Pull up the thread ends to gather the edges of all the petals, then join the first petal to the last and fasten off the thread securely.

7 Using strong thread, sew a running stitch all around the circle that you set aside in step 1, leaving a tail of thread at each end of the stitching.

8 Place the outer part of the self-covering button on the wrong side of this circle and pull up the ends of the thread to gather the fabric; fasten off securely. Press the back of the button in place.

9 Place the button in the centre of the cluster of petals and slipstitch (see page 15) the edge of the button to the flower.

10 Cut a circle of felt measuring $1\frac{1}{2}$in (4cm) in diameter. Stitch the brooch pin to the centre of the circle.

11 Place the felt circle on the back of the corsage, in the centre. Oversew the edges to secure it in place.

Tip

Depending on the thickness of the fabric, the hole in the centre after you've gathered the petals might be larger or smaller than that shown in step 6 or it might be completely closed. This will affect the size of the finished corsage.

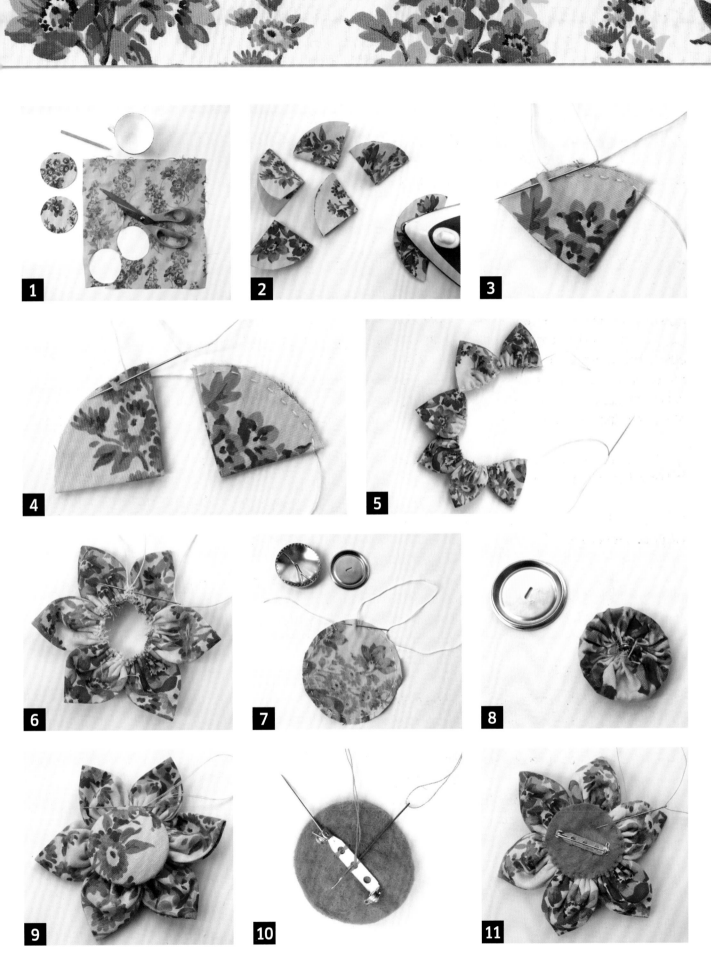

SEWING MACHINE COVER

Whether you use an antique sewing machine or a modern one, this accessory is a useful addition to the sewing room. Place it over your sewing machine when it's not in use, to protect it from knocks and keep it dust-free.

Find the template on page 135

You will need
2 fat quarters of vintage printed cotton fabric
2 fat quarters of plain cotton fabric, for lining
Cotton wadding (batting),
    at least 29½ x 18in (75 x 45cm)
3½yd (3.25m) of 1in (2cm) bias binding
Pencil or fabric marker
Paper for pattern
Pins
Binder clips (optional)
Dressmaking scissors
Sewing machine
Sewing needle
Thread for tacking (basting)
Thread to match fabric
Iron and ironing board

NOTE: The seams on this cover are on the outside; they are covered with bias binding for a neat and eye-catching finish.

Finished size:
Will fit most standard sewing machines but see note on page 52

NOTE: Before you start, measure your sewing machine to make sure the cover will fit. First, measure the length of the machine, making sure you include the wheel on the right-hand side; this should be no longer than 17in (43cm). Measure the width at the widest point; this should be no wider than $8\frac{1}{4}$in (21cm). Now place one end of the tape measure on the work surface at the back of the machine and bring it right over the top to the front, ending at the work surface again; this measurement should be no longer than $28\frac{1}{2}$in (72cm). If your machine is larger than this, you will need to enlarge the pattern pieces and you will need more than two fat quarters of both the main fabric and the lining.

1 Make a paper pattern for the side panels, using the template on page 135. Cut a rectangle measuring $17\frac{3}{4}$ x 14in (45 x 35.5cm) from each of the printed and plain fat quarters. Stack the remaining fabrics together and pin the pattern for side panels of the cover towards the top. Cut out through all four layers. Trim the remaining fabric to 8 x $6\frac{1}{2}$in (20.5 x 16.5cm); these pieces will form the pockets at each end of the cover.

2 Machine stitch the two large rectangles of printed fabric along one of their long edges with a $\frac{3}{8}$in (1cm) seam allowance. Press the seam open. Repeat with the two lining pieces.

3 Cut a piece of wadding (batting) measuring $17\frac{3}{4}$ x $27\frac{1}{4}$in (45 x 69cm). Sandwich the wadding between the patterned and plain pieces joined in step 2, with the right sides of the fabrics facing outwards. Tack (baste) all around, keeping your stitches within the seam allowance.

4 Cut two pieces of wadding using the side panel pattern. Sandwich the wadding between the patterned fabric and lining pieces, with the right sides of fabrics facing outwards. Pin and/or tack around the curved edge.

5 Place the pocket pieces together with their corresponding linings, wrong sides together. Bind one long edge of each, using the one-step method described on page 20.

6 Place the pockets on the side panels, matching the lower (straight) edges. Pin together, then tack all around, keeping your stitches within the seam allowance and stitching through all thicknesses.

7 Bind the lower edges of the main piece and both side panels, using the one-step method.

8 Pin the side panels to the main piece, matching the lower edges and easing the long edge of the main piece around the curve at the top of each side panel. Instead of pins, you may find it easier to use clips for this. Tack, then machine stitch.

9 Bind the seams you've just stitched, using the two-step method described on page 20.

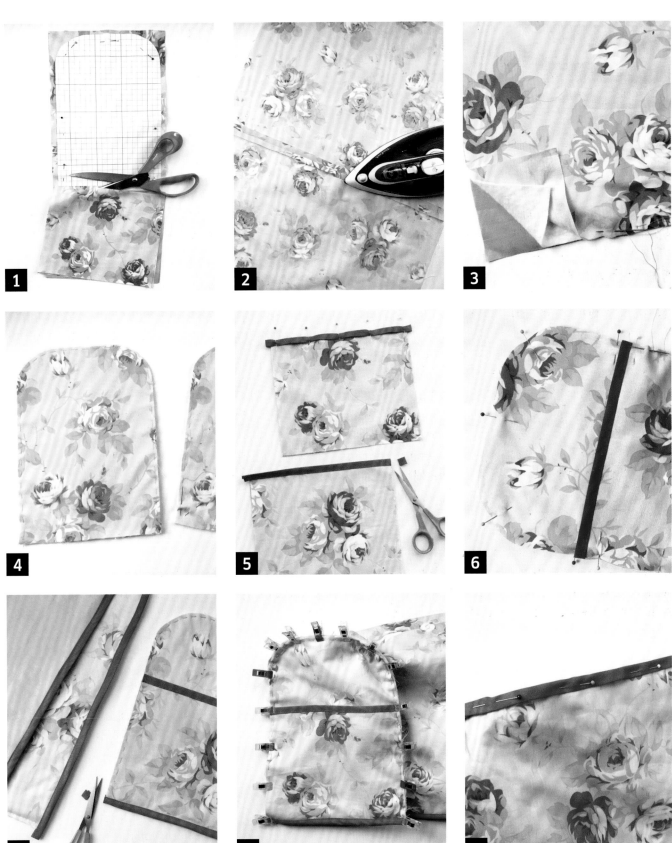

COAT HANGER COVER

Vintage clothes need special care. Protect the shoulders of a cherished dress, blouse or jacket with a custom-made cover. Hang your garment on a padded hanger to cushion the shoulders, then slip the cover over it to keep it free from dust and grime.

Find the template on page 136

You will need
1 fat quarter of vintage printed cotton fabric
1 fat quarter of plain cotton fabric, for lining
40in (1m) of cotton lace edging or broderie anglaise,
    approximately 3–4in (7–10cm) wide
Pencil or fabric marker
Paper for making pattern
Pins
Dressmaking scissors
General-purpose scissors
Sewing machine
Sewing needle
Thread for tacking (basting)
Thread to match fabric
Iron and ironing board

Finished size is roughly:
36 x 26in (91 x 66cm)

1 Make a paper pattern from the template on page 136. Cut two pieces from the vintage printed fabric and two from the plain cotton lining fabric.

2 Cut the lace edging or broderie anglaise into two equal lengths. Pin one length to the straight edge of each of the printed fabric pieces, with a slight overlap at each end; the unfinished edge of the lace should go along the straight edge of the fabric. Machine stitch in place ³/₈in (1cm) from the edge of the fabric.

3 Press the seams to one side, away from the lace edging.

4 Place the two lace-trimmed pieces right sides together, matching the edges. Mark a gap at the top, in the centre, by placing pins 2in (5cm) apart. Pin and tack (baste) around the curved top and sides.

5 Machine stitch the pieces together, leaving the 2in (5cm) gap unstitched. Snip into the seam allowance around the curve. Repeat steps 4 and 5 with the two lining pieces.

6 Neaten the raw edges of the lace edging with a narrow double hem, slipstitching (see page 15) the folded edge to the seam line.

7 On the lower (straight) edge of the lining, press ³/₈in (1cm) to the wrong side.

8 Along the gap at the centre top of both the main piece and the lining, fold the raw edges to the wrong side and press. Turn the main piece right side out. Place the lining inside the cover, so that the wrong sides are together. Line up the openings at the centre top and slipstitch the folded edges together.

9 On the lower edge, on the inside of the cover, slipstitch the folded edge of the lining to the seam line of the lace, covering the raw edge of the lace.

Tip

Cotton lace edging with one unfinished edge is best for this project. If, however, you cut the pieces for your cover from fabric with a hemmed edge, you could leave it as it is or choose a lace trim with a finished edge and slipstitch it to the edge of the hem.

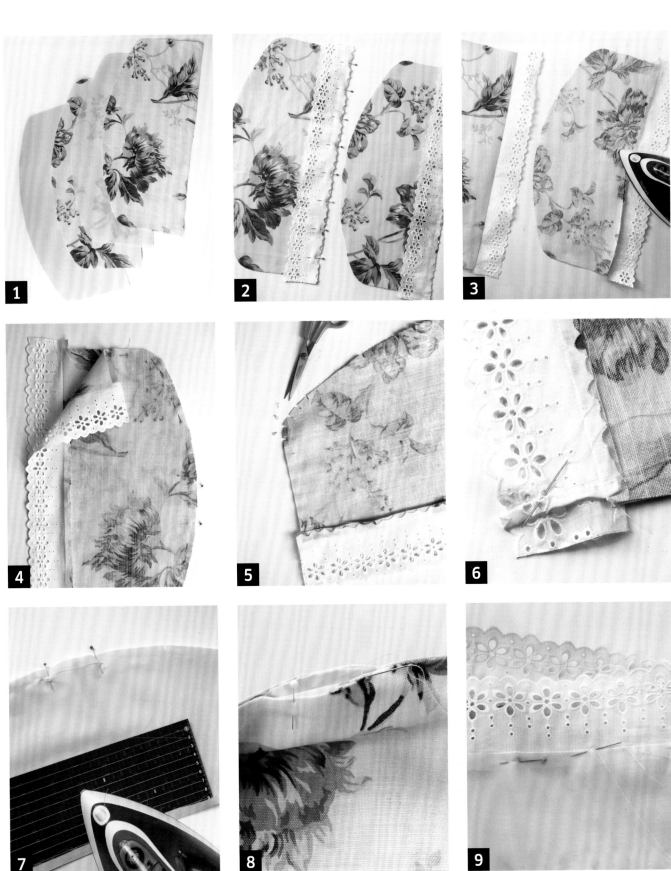

PEG BAG

For previous generations, washday was a chore. Washing machines were a rarity: people were more likely to use a washtub, a washboard for scrubbing out stains and grime, and a mangle for squeezing out the excess water before hanging the washing to dry in the breeze, pegged to a line. And this little peg bag would have been the ideal place to store the pegs and keep them at hand.

Find the template on page 137

You will need
1 fat quarter of vintage printed fabric
1 fat quarter of plain fabric, for lining
Lightweight wadding (batting), approx. 20 x 15in (51 x 38cm)
4ft (1.2m) of $\frac{5}{8}$in- (15mm-) wide printed bias binding
Coat hanger
Pencil or fabric marker
Paper for making pattern
Pins
Dressmaking scissors
General-purpose scissors
Sewing machine
Sewing needle
Thread for tacking (basting)
Thread to match fabric
Iron and ironing board

Finished size is roughly:
Approx. 10in (25cm) deep and 13in (33cm) wide.

1 Make a paper pattern, using the template on page 137 (see page 14). Fold the main fabric and lining in half and place them on top of each other, with the folded edges aligned. Place the lower (straight) edge of the paper pattern on the fold and pin it in place. Cut out.

2 Open out the fabric and re-pin the pattern to one of the curved edges, then cut out the curved shape that's marked at the top of the pattern, cutting through both the main fabric and lining.

3 Cut out the same shape from wadding (batting), using one of the fabric pieces as a template. Sandwich the wadding between the fabric pieces, with the right sides facing out. Pin, then tack (baste) the layers together.

4 Machine stitch all round, ¼in (6mm) from the edges. Trim the wadding close to the stitch line.

5 Cut a length of binding slightly longer than the curved edge. Lining up the raw edge of the binding with the edge of the fabrics, backstitch (see page 17) along the crease by hand.

6 Fold the binding to the inside and slipstitch (see page 15) the folded edge to the stitch line. Trim the ends of the binding flush with the top of the fabric piece.

7 Fold the piece in half, matching the top (curved) edges and the sides. Machine stitch the side seams with a ¼in (6mm) seam allowance. Trim the edges, if necessary.

8 Use the remaining binding to bind the two side edges, using the two-step method described on page 20. When you come to the top of this edge, snip into the binding and ease the binding around the corner.

9 Fold the binding to the back and slipstitch the folded edge in place.

10 Press the binding. Place the coat hanger inside to complete your project.

Tip

Check that the pattern fits your coat hanger. Line up the top edge of the coat hanger with the top of the pattern and, if necessary, trace a line along the top of the hanger and trim the pattern along this line.

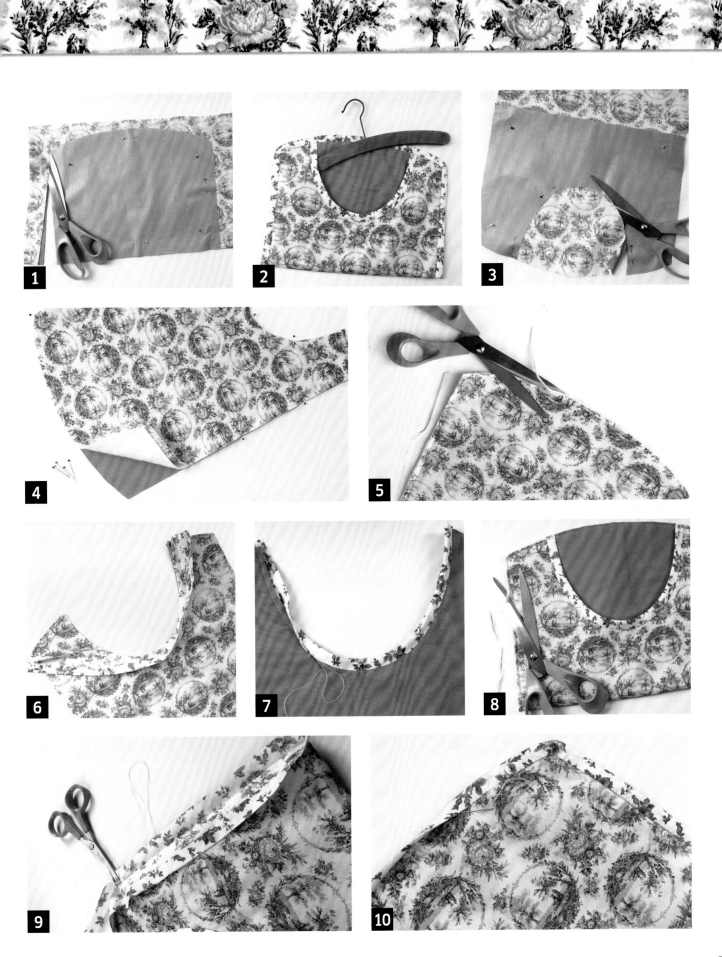

PATCHWORK COT QUILT

The idea of using small scraps of fabric to make a colourful quilt fits in with the ethos of 'make do and mend'. This cot-sized quilt is inspired by a larger World War Two quilt made by the Methodist Ladies of New York and sent to Britain.

Find the template on page 137

Find the template on page 137

You will need
Scraps of vintage printed fabric in various different prints
1yd (1m) plain cotton fabric, for lining
Cotton wadding (batting), 37½ x 27in (93 x 67 cm)
Quilter's pencil or erasable fabric marker
Card or plastic, for making template
Pins
Dressmaking scissors
General-purpose scissors
Sewing machine
Sewing needle
Thread for tacking (basting)
Thread to match fabric
Iron and ironing board

NOTE: Each square measures 6in (15cm).

Tip

Instead of buying fabric specially, the patchwork can be made from oddments and pieces left over from other projects, in the spirit of making use of every little scrap and not letting anything go to waste.

During World War Two, hundreds of thousands of quilts made by Canadian women were sent to Britain and distributed to people who had lost their possessions in bombing raids, and to hospitals, convalescent homes and children's nurseries. Each quilt had a small label that read 'Gift of Canadian Red Cross' who organized this scheme.

Finished size is roughly:
36 x 25½in (91 x 66cm)

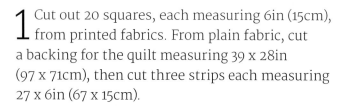

1 Cut out 20 squares, each measuring 6in (15cm), from printed fabrics. From plain fabric, cut a backing for the quilt measuring 39 x 28in (97 x 71cm), then cut three strips each measuring 27 x 6in (67 x 15cm).

2 Join the squares together in four strips of five patches each, with a $^3/_8$in (1cm) seam allowance. Press the seams to one side.

3 Alternating plain fabric strips and patchwork strips, join the strips along the long edges. Press the seams towards the patchwork strips.

4 Layer the quilt: place the backing wrong side up on the work surface with the wadding (batting) centred on top and the patchwork right side up on top of the wadding. The wadding is now sandwiched between the fabrics. Pin all round, then tack (baste) with large stitches, working from the centre outwards, with lines of tacking about 4–5in (10–12cm) apart.

5 Sew running stitch along the seam lines, through all layers; this is known as 'quilting in the ditch'.

6 Lay the quilt on a flat surface. Cut a template (see page 137) from cardboard or plastic. Starting at the centre of one plain strip, and placing the long straight edge of the template along a seam line, draw along the wavy edge using an erasable pencil or pen. Repeat on all the plain strips, on both edges.

7 Sew running stitch along the lines you have drawn, taking the needle through all the layers. The length of the stitches is not important, but they should be as even as possible for a neat result.

8 Remove the tacking stitches. Fold the raw edge of the backing fabric over to meet the raw edge of the patchwork. Press.

9 Unfold the pressed-over backing fabric, then trim off the four corners, $^3/_8$in (1cm) from the corner of the patchwork.

10 Fold the trimmed corner over the corner of the patchwork, then fold the edges over again, bringing the first fold over onto the patchwork, to form a narrow border. Press.

11 Pin the border in place, paying particular attention to the mitred corners.

12 Slipstitch (see page 15) the folded edge of the border in place. At each corner, slipstitch the folded edges of the mitred corners together.

Tip

To make the quilting template, you can use medium-weight card – or look out for sheets of plastic (polypropylene) marked with a grid, specially designed for cutting patterns and templates that can be used time and time again without the edges becoming distressed.

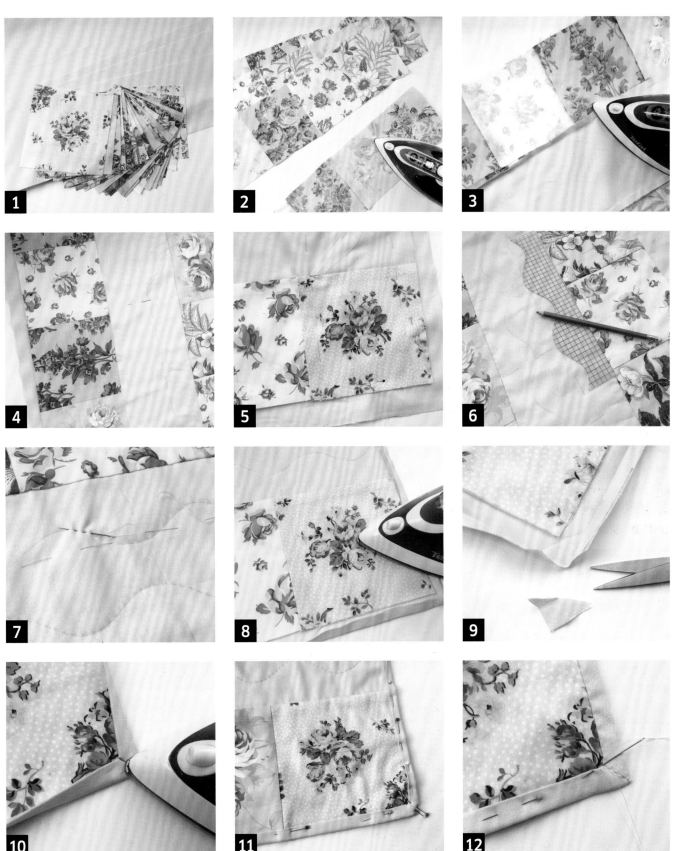

1950s

TABLE RUNNER

Use this project to showcase a favourite Fifties fabric, combining it with a co-ordinating modern print. The finished runner can be used down the centre of the dining table or perhaps on a sideboard. It also makes a lovely picnic cloth.

You will need
1 fat quarter of vintage printed cotton fabric
2 fat quarters of co-ordinating printed cotton fabric
4¼yd (3.75m) of ¾in (2cm) bias binding
Tailor's chalk or chalk pencil
Pins
Dressmaking scissors
Pinking shears
Sewing machine
Sewing needle
Thread for tacking (basting)
Thread to match fabric
Iron and ironing board

NOTE: This 1950s fabric, with its stylized bottles, glasses, food and utensils, is typical of the pictorial prints of this period. The companion print is more modern and has been chosen because it has a retro feel, and because the colours are a good match.

Tip
You will find many online sellers offering vintage fabrics cut into fat quarters. This project is designed to make the most of a vintage fat quarter with very little waste.

Finished size is roughly:
56¾ x 17in (144 x 43cm)

1 From the vintage fabric, cut two rectangles measuring 21⅝ x 8¾in (55 x 22cm). Cut the same from one of the co-ordinating fat quarters; from the other, cut three strips measuring 17½ x 7in (44 x 18cm).

2 Pair the large pieces of vintage fabric with the co-ordinating pieces and join each pair along one long edge with a ⅜in (1cm) seam allowance. Alternate the order of the fabrics – so that one pair has the vintage print at the top and the other has the co-ordinating print at the top.

Tip

If your fabric has a directional print, make sure it's facing the same way in each pair.

3 Trim the seams with pinking shears, to prevent fraying.

4 Press the seams open.

5 Place a small strip in between the two larger pieces and stitch together with a ⅜in (1cm) seam allowance. Stitch the two remaining strips to the other short edges of the larger pieces. Trim the short strips, if necessary, so that they're level with the larger pieces. Trim the seams with pinking shears and press them open.

6 Place an object approximately 4¾in (12cm) in diameter on each corner and draw around it with tailor's chalk; cut out along the lines you have drawn.

Tip

The corners of the runner are rounded, making it easier to apply the bias binding. Sewing the binding by hand gives a neat result, but you may prefer to stitch it by machine.

7 Topstitch (see page 19) along each side of all the seams, about ⅛in (3mm) from the seam line.

8 Bind the edge with bias binding. Starting on the right side, open out the binding and line up the raw edge with the edge of the runner, then backstitch (see page 17) along the fold.

9 Fold the binding over the edge to the wrong side. Pin all around, then slipstitch (see page 15) the folded edge of the binding to the line of backstitch; press.

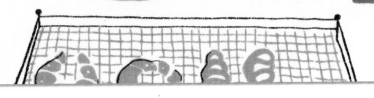

1

2

3

4
5
6

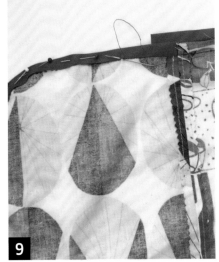

7
8
9

TEA COSY

In the good old days, tea wasn't made with a tea bag in a mug – it was made in a teapot and left to brew before pouring, so a tea cosy was essential to keep it nice and hot. This tea cosy features a vintage 1950s print – 'Flowerpots' by John Murray for David Whitehead – and a bright, co-ordinating lining.

Find the template on page 138

You will need
1 fat quarter of vintage printed cotton fabric
1 fat quarter of plain cotton fabric, for lining
¼yd (25cm) of medium-weight wadding (batting)
6in (15cm) of ⅝in (15mm) cotton tape
Paper for pattern
Quilter's pencil or chalk pencil
Pins
Dressmaking scissors
General-purpose scissors
Sewing machine
Sewing needle
Seam gauge (optional)
Thread for tacking (basting)
Strong thread for quilting
Thread to match fabric
Iron and ironing board

Finished size:
Fits a medium-sized teapot

1 Using the template on page 138, make two paper patterns (see page 14). Cut along the marked line on one pattern to make a shorter pattern for the outer cosy. Use the shorter pattern to cut two pieces from printed fabric and wadding (batting), and the larger one to cut two pieces from plain fabric.

2 Place a piece of wadding on the wrong side of each printed fabric piece and tack (baste) the two layers together using large stitches.

3 Draw vertical lines ¾in (2cm) apart, across the width of the fabric.

4 Using strong thread, sew lines of running stitch along the lines you have drawn, taking the needle through both layers.

5 Fold the cotton tape in half and place the ends level with the top of one of the quilted pieces, in the centre; stitch in place.

6 Pin the two quilted pieces right sides together, lining up the edges, and stitch together with a ⅜in (1cm) seam all round the curved edge, by hand or by machine, leaving the lower (straight) edge unstitched.

7 Trim away the excess wadding, close to the stitch line. Snip into the seam allowance on curves. Turn right side out.

8 Repeat step 6 with the two lining pieces. Snip into the seam allowance around the curves. To create a hem on the lower edge, turn ⅜in (1cm) to the wrong side and press, then turn a further 1¼in (3cm) to the wrong side and press again.

9 Place the lining inside the tea cosy, wrong sides together. Bring the hem on the lining to the right side, pin in place and slipstitch (see page 15) the fold to the outer part of the cover.

10 With matching thread, sew two parallel lines of running stitch approximately ³⁄₁₆in and ⅜in (5mm and 10mm) from the edge, through all layers.

Tip

A seam gauge is a great little tool for pressing accurate hems.

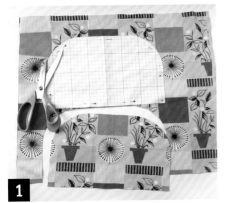

1

2

3

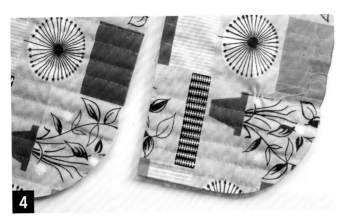

4

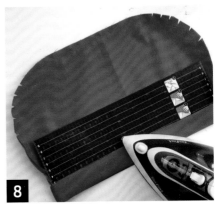

5

6

7

8

9

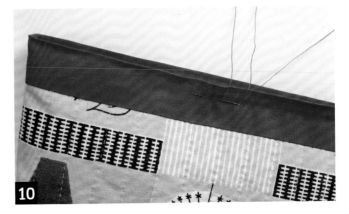

10

APRON

In the 1950s, a 'pinny' wasn't just something to wear while cooking, to protect your clothes – it was a fashion statement. This one features a front panel of vintage fabric combined with a woven check and a contrasting plain fabric, all gathered into a waistband that ties in a flamboyant bow at the back.

Find the template on page 139

You will need
1 fat quarter of vintage printed cotton or linen fabric
1 fat quarter of woven checked cotton fabric
60in (150cm) plain cotton or linen
Three 55in (1.4m) lengths of ric-rac braid
Pencil or fabric marker
Paper for making pattern
Pins
Dressmaking scissors
General-purpose scissors
Sewing machine
Sewing needle
Thread for tacking (basting)
Thread to match fabric
Iron and ironing board
Hem gauge (optional)

NOTE: Ric-rac – sometimes spelt rickrack – dates back to the mid-19th century and is useful for edging and trimming. This pretty zigzag braid is practical and durable, perfect for decorating items like this apron, that need to be laundered frequently. It is readily available, inexpensive and comes in a range of colours and widths.

Finished size is roughly:
Width at hem: 39³/₈in (100cm),
Length: 26³/₈in (67cm),
Sash: 6ft 7in (2m) long

1 Trim the two fat quarters to measure $21^5/8$ x $17^3/4$in (55 x 45cm). Cut the checked fabric in half, to produce two pieces measuring $8^7/8$ x $17^3/4$in (22.5 x 45cm).

2 Join the checked fabric to the printed fabric along the long edges, with a $3/8$in (1cm) seam allowance, placing the printed fabric in the centre and the checked fabric on either side. Press the seams open.

3 From the plain fabric, cut a piece measuring $37^3/8$ x $10^1/4$in (96 x 26cm) for the lower border. Stitch this to the lower edge of the pieces you stitched together in step 2, again with a $3/8$in (1cm) seam allowance. Trim the sides level with those of the pieced section. Press the seam open.

4 Stitch a length of ric-rac braid across the top of the plain band approximately $3/8$in (1cm) below the seam line, and stitch two further lengths below this and parallel to it about $1^1/4$–$1^1/2$in (3–4cm) apart. Trim off the excess braid at each end.

5 Hem both sides of the apron: fold $3/8$in (1cm) to the wrong side, then a further $5/8$in (1.5cm), to form a double hem. Press, then stitch by hand or by machine. For the bottom hem, turn $3/8$in (1cm) to the wrong side, then a further $1^1/4$in (3cm). Press, then slipstitch (see page 15) the folded edge in place.

6 From the plain fabric, cut two pieces measuring 17 x 7in (43 x 18cm) for the pockets. Fold each piece in half across its width to find the centre; press. Open out each one and stitch three lengths of ric-rac braid to each, placing the first one approximately $3/8$in (1cm) below the fold and the others below this and parallel to it, about $1^1/4$–$1^1/2$in (3–4cm) apart. Trim off any excess braid at each side.

7 Fold the pockets in half with right sides together. Mark a gap on the short (unfolded) edge by placing pins approximately 4in (10cm) apart. Machine stitch around three sides (excluding the folded edge), leaving the space between the pins unstitched. Clip the corners (see page 21) and turn the pockets right side out.

8 Pin the pockets on the apron, across the seams, with the top of each pocket about 2in (5cm) above the seam line on the border. Machine stitch in place, stitching down the sides and across the base.

9 From the remaining plain fabric, cut a strip measuring 28 x $6^1/4$in (72 x 16cm), across the whole width of the fabric, for the waistband. Then, using the template on page 139, cut two tie ends from the remaining fabric. Stitch a tie end to each short end of the long strip. Press the seams open, then press $3/8$in (1cm) to the wrong side on both long edges. To help with this, use a hem gauge.

10 Fold the piece in half lengthways and, starting from each end in turn, sew along the short end then down the length, leaving the centre 24in (60cm) open. Clip the corners at each end and turn right side out.

11 Sew two lines of stitching across the top of the apron. Place the first line $3/16$in (5mm) from the raw edge and the second line $3/16$in (5mm) below that, leaving a tail of thread at each end so you've got something to pull. Pull up the ends of the thread to gather the fabric until the top edge measures 24in (60cm). Adjust the gathers so that they are even.

12 Insert the gathered edge of the apron into the gap in the sash. Pin it in place, then slipstitch the folded edges of the sash to the fabric, on both the right side and on the reverse.

SPECTACLE CASE

This neat little slipcase, made from a pretty gingham fabric and decorated with a bow, will protect your glasses or sunglasses from getting scratched. Pop it into your bag or into the pocket of a shirt or jacket, to keep your specs handy.

You will need
1 fat quarter of woven cotton gingham fabric
Fusible fleece, 8 x 7in (20 x 18cm)
4in (10cm) length of ¼in (6mm) elastic
Self-covering button, 1⅛in (29mm) in diameter
Pencil or fabric marker
Pins
Dressmaking scissors
General-purpose scissors
Sewing machine
Sewing needle
Thread for tacking (basting)
Thread to match fabric
Iron and ironing board
Non-stick baking parchment
Corner and edge shaper or similar tool,
    such as a knitting needle

Finished size:
7 x 4in (18 x 10cm)

1 Cut two rectangles of gingham fabric measuring 9½ x 8in (24 x 20cm).

2 Cut a piece of fusible fleece measuring 8 x 7in (20 x 18cm). Place it centrally on the wrong side of one of the pieces of gingham and fuse it in place with a hot iron, protecting the base plate with a sheet of non-stick baking parchment.

3 Fold the elastic in half and pin the two ends to one long edge of one of the gingham pieces, on the right side, 2½in (6cm) from the corner, with the loop pointing in. Place the other piece of gingham on top, right sides together, and pin.

4 Mark a gap on one short side by placing pins 3–4in (8–10cm) apart. Machine stitch all around with a ¼in (6mm) seam allowance, leaving the gap between the pins unstitched. Snip off the corners.

5 Turn the case right side out and push out the corners using a corner and edge shaper or similar tool.

6 Turn the seam allowance to the inside along the edges of the gap, then press.

7 Fold the piece in half, right sides together, matching the short edges. Pin or clip, then stitch around the side and base, with a ¼in (6mm) seam allowance. Turn right side out.

8 To make the bow, cut a rectangle of fabric measuring 11¾ x 4⅜in (30 x 11cm). Fold the strip in half lengthways and stitch down the length with a ¼in (6mm) seam allowance. Turn right side out, flatten it out so that the seam runs down the centre and press. On each end, turn ⅜in (1cm) to the inside, and press again.

9 Join the two short ends by slipstitching (see page 15) the folded edges together.

10 Bring the join to the centre and bind it tightly with thread to create a bow shape.

11 Cut a circle of fabric 2in (5cm) in diameter. Sew a running stitch all around the edge. Place the outer part of the self-covering button in the centre and pull up the thread to gather the fabric. Fasten off, then place the button back on top and snap it in place.

12 Stitch the centre of the bow to the front of the spectacle case, in the centre, then sew the button to the centre of the bow.

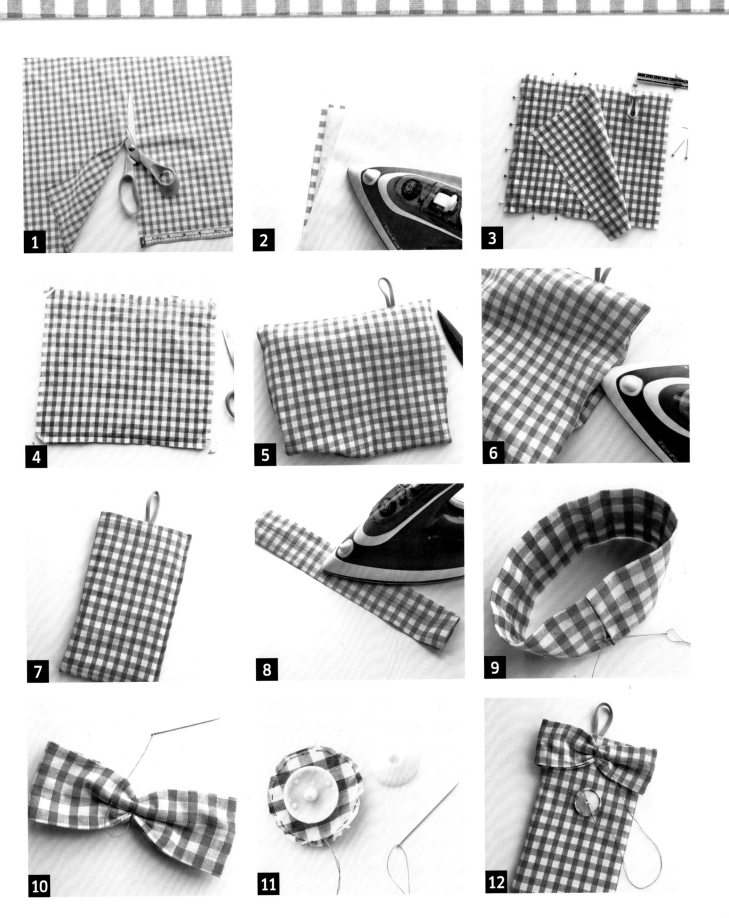

HOT-WATER BOTTLE COVER

Back in the Fifties, it was unusual for houses to be centrally heated – so on cold winter nights a hot-water bottle in a cosy cover, slipped between the sheets, helped to keep your toes nice and warm as you drifted off to sleep.

Find the template on page 140

Finished size is roughly:
14 x 9in (35.5 x 23cm)

You will need
1 fat quarter of printed cotton fabric
1 fat quarter of plain cotton fabric
1 fat quarter of fusible fleece
20in (50cm) length of ¾in (2cm) bias binding
Pencil or fabric marker
Paper for making pattern
Pins
Dressmaking scissors
Pinking shears
General-purpose scissors
Sewing machine
Sewing needle
Thread for tacking (basting)
Thread to match fabric
Iron and ironing board
Non-stick baking parchment

NOTE: Throughout the 1950s, novelty printed fabrics of all kinds were popular. As well as a plethora of geometric patterns, picture prints were inspired by all kinds of themes, from foreign travel to mythology, and from animals and nature to science, technology and outer space.

1 Make paper patterns from the template on page 140 (see page 14). Place the plain and patterned fat quarters together, place the patterns on top, and pin through all layers. Cut out the fabric pieces.

NOTE: When placing the pattern pieces, take the design of the fabric into account before cutting.

2 Using the same paper patterns, cut one of each piece from fusible fleece. Trim away $5/16$in (8mm) all round from each fleece piece, then apply these to the corresponding pieces of printed fabric. Fuse in place with a hot iron, protecting the base plate with a sheet of non-stick baking parchment.

3 Place the corresponding pieces of main fabric and lining together, right sides out, and tack (baste) all round, keeping the stitching within the seam allowance.

4 Bind the straight edge of each of the smaller pieces, using the one-step method described on page 20. These will form the back of the hot-water bottle cover.

5 Place the front piece right side up. Place the top back piece on top, right side down, lining up the edges, then place the lower back piece on top, lining up the bottom and side edges. The two back pieces will overlap slightly. Pin the layers together.

6 Machine stitch all around, $3/8$in (1cm) from the edge. Trim the seam allowance using pinking shears.

7 Turn the cover right side out through the gap between the bound edges.

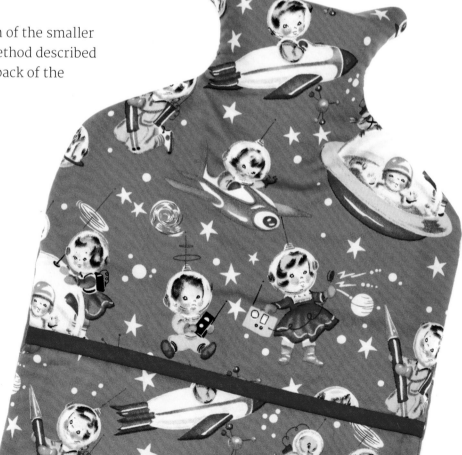

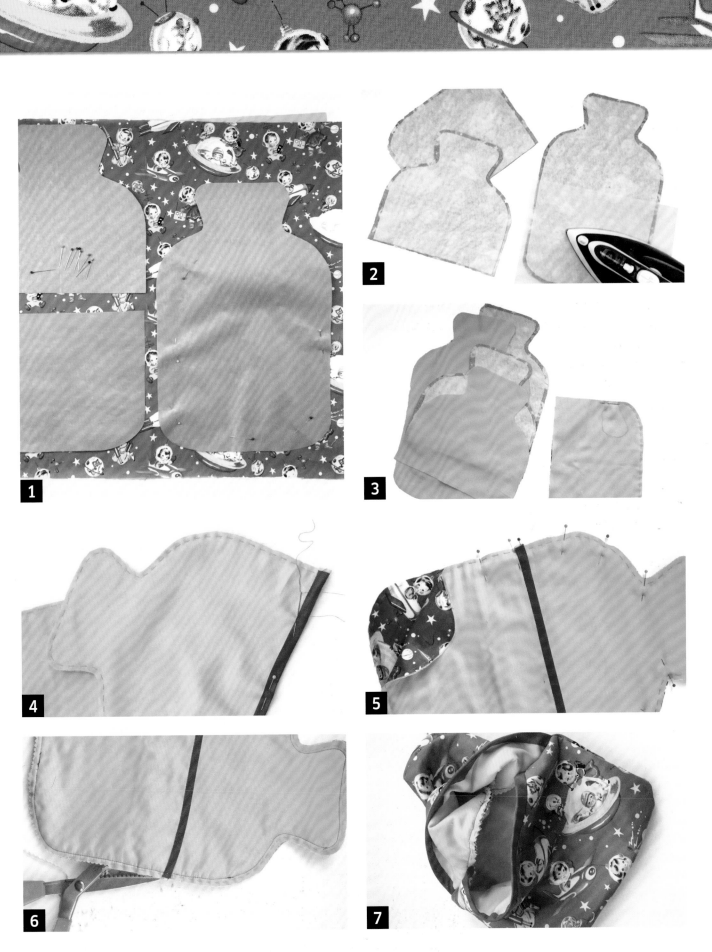

1960s

APPLIQUÉ CUSHION

In the Sixties, a sofa – sometimes called a 'studio couch' back then – wasn't complete without a pile of scatter cushions. Make your own pair of flower-power pillows with 1960s fabric – real or reproduction – and an eye-catching appliqué.

Find the templates on pages 141–142

You will need
2 fat quarters of plain cotton fabric
Small pieces of fabric in four different colours, for appliqué (see step 1 for amounts)
Small pieces of fusible bonding web, for appliqué
50in (1.3m) length of bobble braid
12in (30cm) square cushion pad
Pencil
Pins
Dressmaking scissors
General-purpose scissors
Sewing machine
Sewing needle
Thread for tacking (basting)
Thread to match fabric
Iron and ironing board
Non-stick baking parchment
Seam gauge (optional)

NOTE: Instructions are given for the appliqué cushion. For the other cushion, replace the appliqué front panel with a square of vintage or repro fabric and back it with plain fabric in a co-ordinating colour.

Tip
In order to cut pieces of plain fabric of the right size for the appliqué cushion cover, you will need two fat quarters. You may, however, prefer to buy a length of fabric from a roll, in which case you will need to buy ½yd (40cm) of fabric 44in or 45in (112cm or 115cm) wide.

Finished size:
12in (30cm) square

1 For the front of the cushion, cut a 12¾in (32cm) square of main fabric from one of the fat quarters; for the back, cut two pieces measuring 12¾ x 8¾in (32 x 22.5cm) from the second fat quarter. For the appliqué, you will need the following colours and approximate sizes of plain cotton fabrics: pink (8in/20cm) square; turquoise (7in/18cm) square; orange (5in/12cm) square; and yellow (2½in/6cm) square.

2 Trace the three flower shapes and the flower centre on pages 141 and 142 onto the paper backing of pieces of fusible bonding web. Cut out roughly.

3 Place the bonding web glue side down on the wrong side of the coloured fabric pieces: the large flower shape on the pink square, the medium-sized flower on the turquoise fabric, the small flower on the orange fabric and the flower centre on the yellow fabric. Fuse in place with a hot iron, placing a piece of non-stick baking parchment on top of the web to protect the base plate of the iron (see page 15).

4 Carefully cut out each of the shapes.

5 Peel off the backing paper from the flower centre and place the yellow circle in the centre of the orange flower. Fuse it in place, then peel away the backing paper from the flower.

6 Using a close machine zigzag stitch (see page 19), stitch all around the flower centre. Pull the thread ends to the wrong side and knot them together, then trim off excess.

7 Place the orange flower on top of the turquoise flower and fuse it in place using a hot iron. Peel off the backing from the turquoise flower and, using a close machine zigzag stitch, stitch all around the edge of the orange flower.

8 Peel off the paper backing from the pink flower and place it in the centre of the plain fabric square. Centre the turquoise flower on top of the pink flower and fuse them in place with a hot iron, then outline both the turquoise and pink flowers with a close machine zigzag, as before.

9 Pin the bobble braid all round the cushion front with the bobbles pointing inwards, easing it round the corners; tack (baste) it in place.

10 On one long edge of each of the back cover pieces, make a double hem by turning ⅜in (1cm) to the wrong side and pressing, then turning a further ⅝in (1.5cm) to the wrong side and pressing again. Stitch.

11 With right sides together, line up the raw edges of the two back pieces with the raw edges of the front panel; the edges that you hemmed in the previous step will overlap. Pin and tack, then machine stitch around all four sides with a ⅜in (1cm) seam allowance, ensuring that the tape of the bobble braid is enclosed within the seam.

12 Clip the corners (see page 21) and turn the cover right side out.

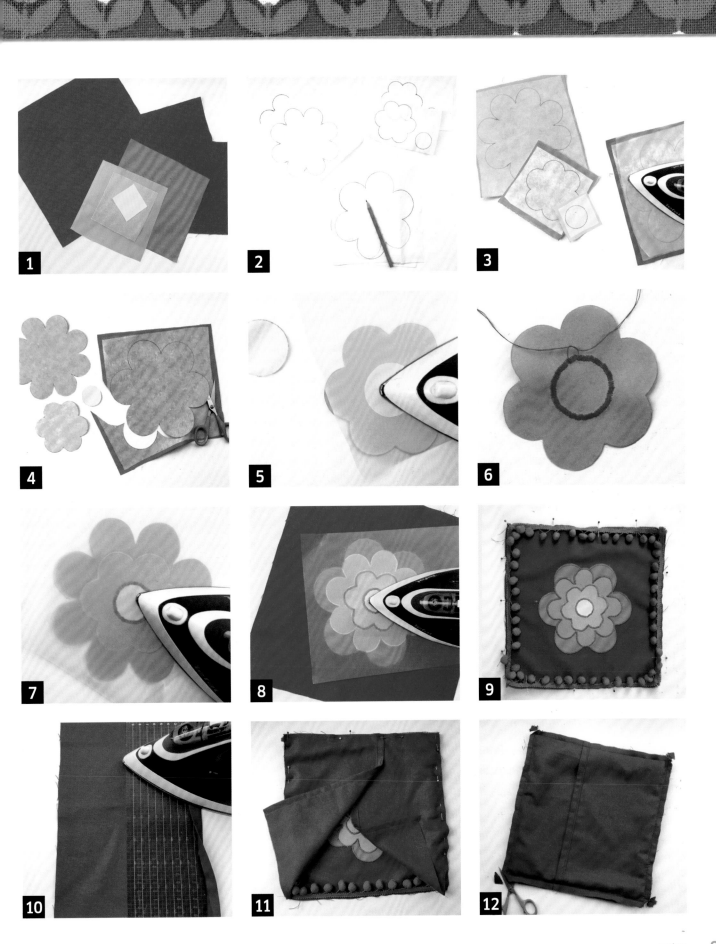

BABY BIB

In the days when doing the laundry was more of a chore, a bib was essential to keep a baby's clothes nice and clean. This one has a stylized cat that is purr-fect for this period – and is quick and easy to embroider in chain stitch, following the outline of the motif.

Find the template on page 143

You will need
1 fat quarter of printed cotton fabric
1 fat quarter of plain cotton fabric
Cotton wadding (batting), approximately 12 x 10in (30 x 25cm)
DMC six-stranded embroidery threads (flosses) in the following colours: blanc (white), 310 (black) and 702 (green)
60in (1.5m) length of $^5/_8$in (15mm) bias binding
Chalk pencil or erasable fabric marker
Thin card for making template
Pins
Embroidery hoop
Dressmaking scissors
Pinking shears
General-purpose scissors
Sewing machine
Sewing needle
Embroidery needle
Thread for tacking (basting)
Thread to match fabric
Iron and ironing board

Finished size is roughly:
10$^1/_2$ x 8in (27 x 20cm)

1 Using the template on page 143, cut a pattern for the pocket from thin card. Place it on the plain fabric, towards the bottom edge, and draw around it with a chalk pencil or erasable fabric marker. Trace the cat motif onto the fabric, in the centre of the shape. Do not cut out at this stage.

2 Place the fabric in an embroidery hoop, with the motif in the centre. Thread the embroidery needle with two strands of white embroidery thread (floss) and begin outlining the cat in chain stitch (see page 16).

3 Continue in chain stitch all around the outline of the cat.

4 Using a single strand of black embroidery thread, embroider the facial features and the line on either side of the cat in backstitch (see page 17).

5 Using two strands of green thread, fill in the bow shape with lines of chain stitch. Once the embroidery is finished, remove the fabric from the hoop and press it on the reverse.

6 Fold the plain fabric in half along the straight line at the top of the pocket, then cut out through both layers. Using the template on page 143, cut two whole bib shapes from printed fabric and one from wadding (batting).

7 Place one printed shape wrong side up, with the wadding on top, then the other printed piece on top, right side up. Place the folded pocket on top. Line up all the edges, pin together and machine stitch all round with a ¼in (6mm) seam allowance. Trim the edges to neaten, if needed.

8 On the front of the bib, stitch binding all round the outer edge, excluding the neckline. Do this by opening up the binding and lining up its edge with the raw edge of the fabric, and backstitching down the creaseline.

9 Turn the bib over. Fold the binding over the edge and pin all round, then slipstitch (see page 15) the folded edge to the line of backstitch.

10 Find the centre of the remaining binding and position it in the centre of the neck. Bind the neckline in the same way as the rest of the bib. The excess binding forms ties: slipstitch the folded edges together and fold in the ends for a neat finish.

Tip

Instead of a plain cotton fabric, you could use towelling or a waterproof material to make the backing of your bib.

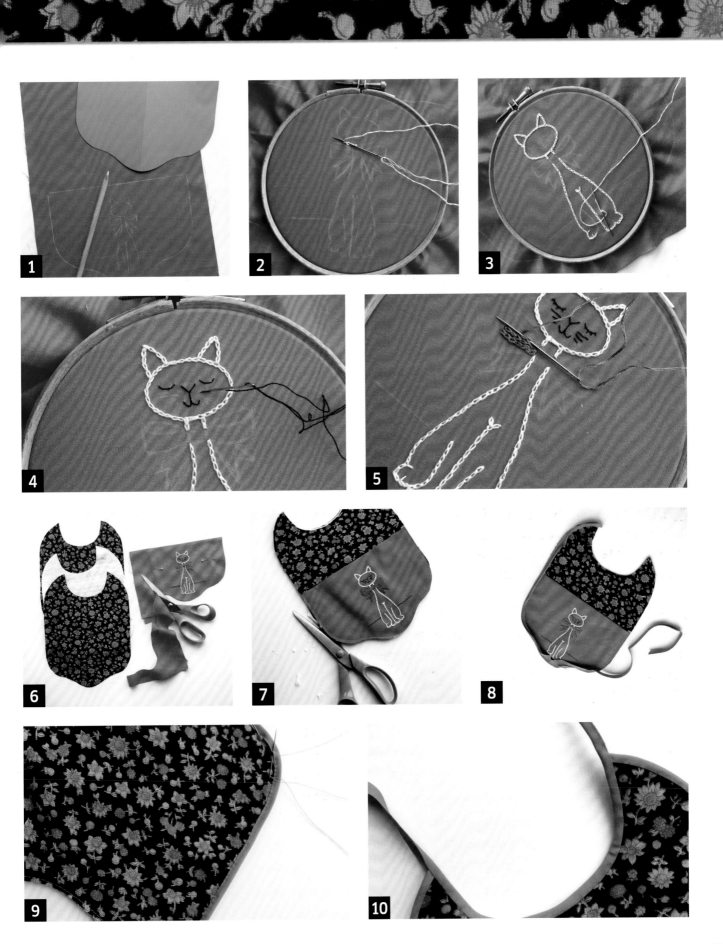

CHILD'S DRESS

In the decade of mini skirts and flamboyant colours, lots of children often wore hand-made clothes. The shapes were simple and the fabrics abundant. This little pinafore dress conjures up the style of the time and is quick and easy to make.

Find the template on page 144

You will need
2 fat quarters of printed cotton fabric
1 fat quarter of plain cotton fabric
25in (63cm) length of ¾in (2cm) bias binding
2yd (2m) of velvet ribbon, ¾in (2cm) wide
Pencil or fabric marker
Card or plastic for making template
Pins
Dressmaking scissors
General-purpose scissors
Sewing machine
Sewing needle
Thread for tacking (basting)
Thread to match fabric
Iron and ironing board

NOTE: Simple and quick to make, this dress is easy enough for a sewing novice. Match the ribbons and binding to the colour of the fabric you are using.

Finished size:
Fits a child aged approximately 3–4 years

1 Place the two fat quarters of printed fabric right sides together. Mark out a rectangle measuring 22 x 18in (55 x 45cm) and cut out.

2 To make the armholes, trace the template on page 144 onto card or plastic and cut it out. Place it on the top corner of the fabric, draw around the curved edge and cut out along the line you have drawn; repeat on the other corner.

3 With right sides together, stitch the side seams with a $^3/_8$in (1cm) seam allowance. Press the seams open.

4 Cut the bias binding into two equal lengths. Open out one edge and stitch it around the armhole on the right side of the fabric, lining up the edge of the binding with the raw edge of the fabric and stitching along the fold line by machine or by hand.

5 Fold the binding to the wrong side, so that the whole width of the tape is on the inside of the armhole, and press.

6 Tack (baste) in place, then stitch close to the edge of the tape. Topstitch (see page 19) about $^1/_8$in (2mm) from the edge of the armhole.

7 On the top edge of the dress, front and back, fold over $^3/_8$in (1cm) and press, then fold over a further 1in (25mm) and press again to make a casing.

8 Stitch the lower edge of the casing, then topstitch about $^1/_8$in (2mm) from the top edge. Cut the ribbon into two equal lengths and thread one piece into each casing.

9 On the lower edge of the dress, turn $^3/_8$in (1cm) to wrong side and press; turn a further $^3/_4$in (2cm) to the wrong side and press again, to make a double hem. Stitch the hem in place.

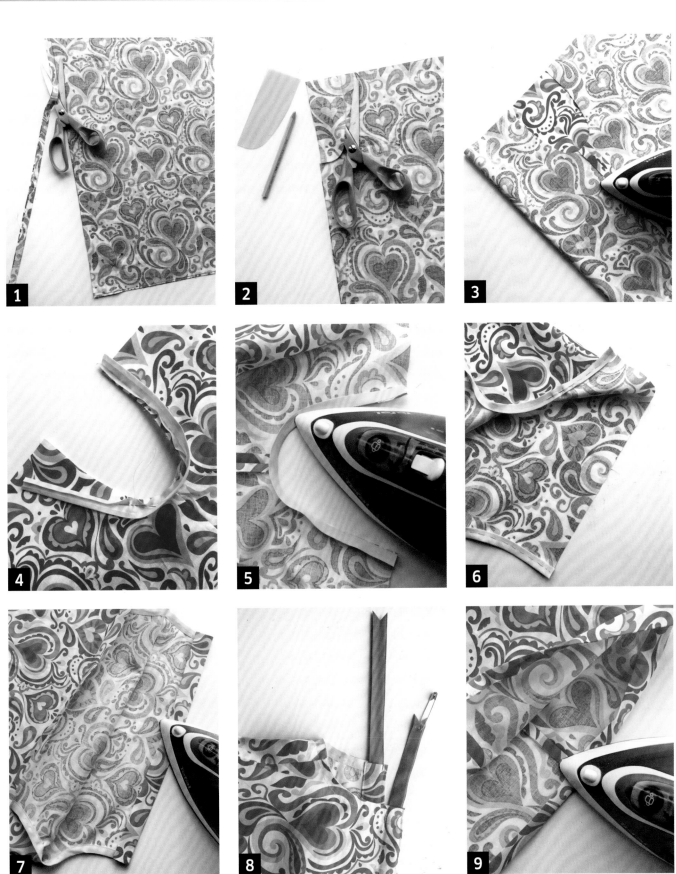

NOTEBOOK COVER

This cover personalizes and protects your notebook. It is also a clever way of utilizing a small fragment of vintage fabric, perhaps rescued from an old dress, combining it with bright plain cotton fabrics, to show it off to its best advantage.

You will need
Small piece of printed cotton fabric,
    at least 9 x 4in (23 x 10cm)
Fat quarters of plain cotton fabric, in two colours
Wadding (batting), at least 13 x 8¾in (33 x 22cm)
A5 notebook
Pencil or fabric marker
Pins
Dressmaking scissors
General-purpose scissors
Corner and edge shaper or similar tool,
    such as a knitting needle
Sewing machine
Sewing needle
Thread to match fabric
Iron and ironing board

Finished size:
Fits an A5 notebook
(5¾ x 8¼in/15 x 21cm)

1 From printed fabric, cut a piece measuring 9 x 4in (23 x 10cm). From one of the plain fabrics (in this case, turquoise blue), cut two pieces for the cover: one measuring 9 x 8¾in (23 x 22.5cm) and the other 9 x 2¼in (23 x 5.5cm). From the other plain fabric (in this case, purple), cut one piece measuring 13½ x 9in (34 x 23cm) for the lining and two pieces measuring 9 x 6¾in (23 x 17cm) for the pockets. From wadding (batting), cut a piece measuring 13 x 8¾in (33 x 22cm).

2 To make the cover, machine stitch the plain and patterned pieces together with a ⅜in (1cm) seam allowance. Press the seams open.

3 To make the pockets, fold each piece in half lengthways, wrong sides together, and press. Sew two lines of topstitching (see page 19) about ³⁄₁₆ and ⅜in (5mm and 10mm) from the folded edge.

4 Place the wadding on the work surface. Place the lining piece right side up on top, and place the pockets on top of this, at either side, lining up the edges. Place the joined cover piece on top, wrong side up.

5 Pin the layers together all around, marking a gap in the centre of the bottom edge by placing pins approximately 5in (12.5cm) apart.

6 Machine stitch all around with a ⅜in (1cm) seam allowance, leaving the gap at the bottom unstitched. Clip the corners (see page 21).

7 Turn right side out, using a corner and edge shaper or similar tool to push out the corners.

8 Turn the seam allowance to the inside along the edges of the gap, then press.

9 Slipstitch (see page 15) the folded edges together to close the gap.

10 Topstitch the cover all around, about ⅛in (3mm) from the edge. Push the covers of the notebook into the pockets on either side.

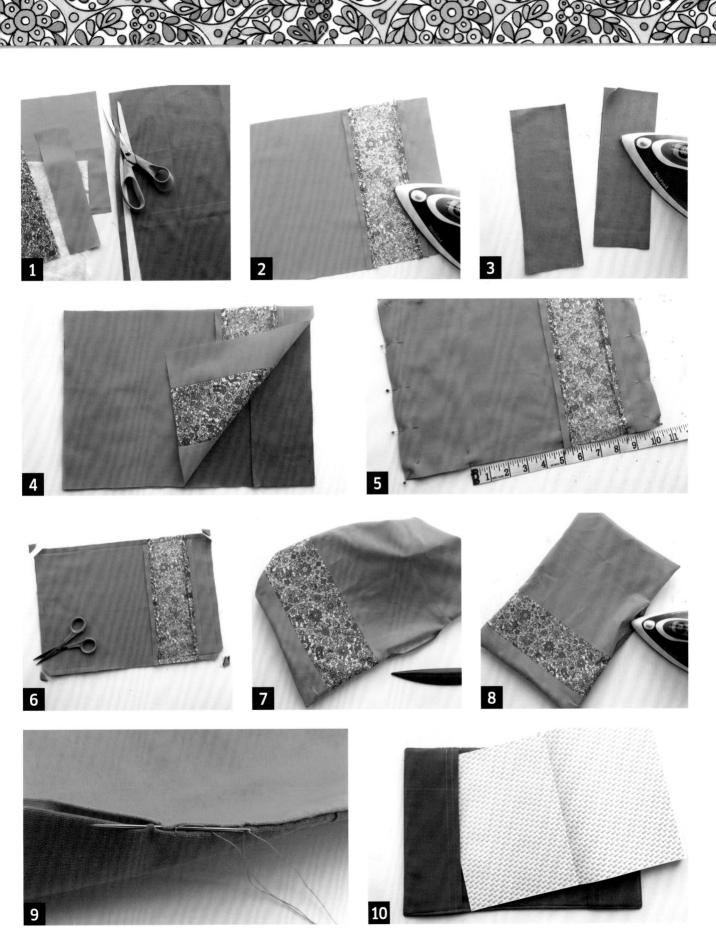

MEMO BOARD

This no-sew project is a good way of showcasing a favourite piece of vintage fabric. The finished board provides a great way of displaying precious old photographs and other memorabilia without sticking pins in them.

You will need
1 fat quarter of printed cotton fabric
Cork board, 15¾ x 11¾in (40 x 30cm)
2¾yd (2.5m) cotton tape, ⅜in (1cm) wide
Tailor's chalk or chalk pencil
Dressmaking scissors
Staple gun
Iron and ironing board
Drawing pins

Tip

This is a no-sew project that is quick and easy to do. The criss-cross tapes hold photos and other items in place. For extra security – and a decorative touch – push drawing pins in at the intersections of the tapes. You will need five pins.

Finished size:
15¾ x 11¾in (40 x 30cm)

1 Place the cork board on the wrong side of the fabric and draw around it, using tailor's chalk in a colour that will show up clearly (in this case, white).

2 Draw a line all around, 1½in (4cm) beyond the first line, to create a border. Cut out the fabric along the outer line.

3 Fold ⅜in (1cm) to the wrong side, all around the edge. Press.

4 Place the cork board face down on the wrong side of the fabric, positioning it centrally. Fold the edge of the fabric over the edge of the board on one long side and staple it in the centre. Do the same with the opposite long edge.

5 Do the same with the two shorter edges, stapling each in the centre of the frame, to hold it in place. Pull the fabric taut as you do this, but do not over-stretch it.

6 Now place staples on either side of the central staple on each long edge. Do the same on the short edges. Then, working outwards towards the corners, place staples about ¾–1¼in (2–3cm) apart, stopping short of the corners, leaving about 3in (7cm) of fabric unstapled.

7 On each corner, fold the corner of the fabric at a right angle, with the point towards the corner of the frame.

8 Bring the fold of fabric over the corner of the board and fix it in place with a staple.

9 Bring up one edge, making sure that the corner is neat, and staple it in place. Do the same with the other edge, then do the same on each corner.

10 Cut two 20in (51cm) lengths of tape and stretch them over the covered board from corner to corner, crossing in the centre. Staple the ends to the sides of the frame. Cut the remaining tape into four equal lengths.

11 Stretch the four lengths of tape across to form a criss-cross pattern on the front of the board.

12 Staple the ends of the tapes to the back of the board, trimming each one and folding under the end of the tape before stapling.

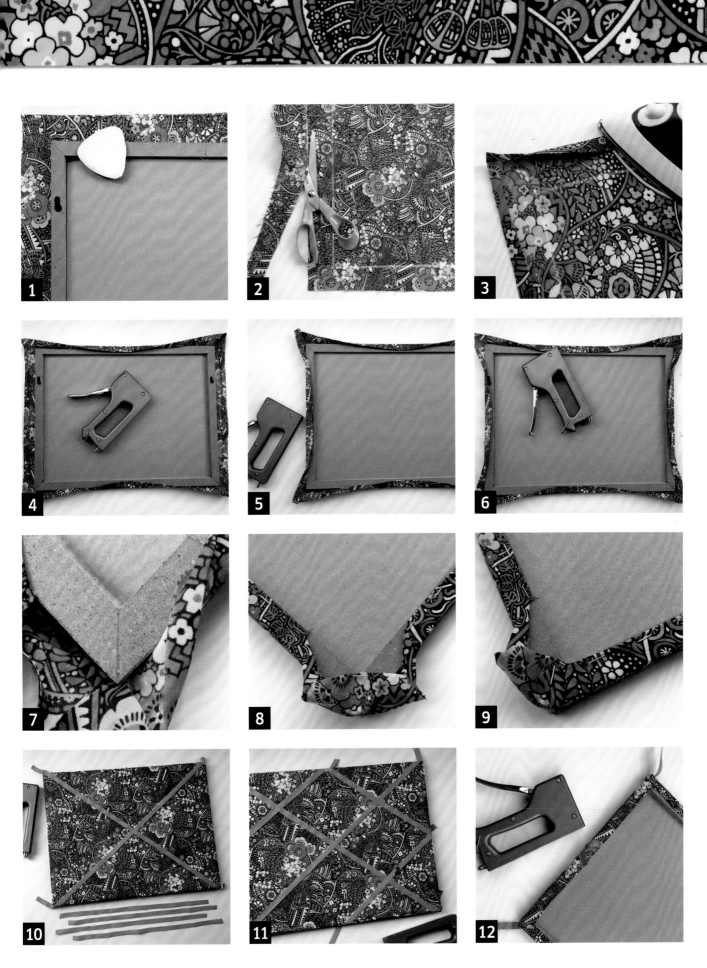

1970s

DRAUGHT EXCLUDER

Cute and practical, this stylized sausage dog, made from vintage 1970s fabric, helps to block draughts and keep your home nice and cosy. For an authentic look, choose a bold print in a typical Seventies colour such as brown, orange or olive green.

Find the templates on pages 144–145

You will need
Printed cotton fabric, at least 34 x 22in (86 x 56cm)
Polyester toy stuffing, about 18–20oz (500–600g)
Two buttons
Tailor's chalk or chalk pencil
Paper for making pattern
Dressmaking scissors
General-purpose scissors
Sewing machine
Sewing needle
Long sewing or upholstery needle
Thread to match fabric
Iron and ironing board

NOTE: Because of its length, the instructions call for a long piece of fabric, at least 32¼in (82cm) long, to accommodate the pattern. You can buy fabric from the roll or you can join four fat quarters – two for each main piece – if you don't mind having a join around the centre of your sausage dog.

Finished size is roughly:
32¼in (82cm) long and 10in (25cm) high

1 Make paper patterns from the templates on pages 144 and 145, joining the two body pieces together to create the full length of the dog's body. Fold the fabric in half, pin each pattern to the double thickness, and cut out two body pieces and four ears.

2 Match two pairs of ears, placing each pair right sides together, and stitch all round the curved edge with a $5/16$in (8mm) seam allowance, leaving the lower (straight) edge open. Snip around the curves.

3 Turn the ears right side out and press with a hot iron.

4 Place the ears in position on the main pieces, with the open edges level with the raw edges of the fabric; pin in place.

5 Place the two main pieces right sides together, with the ears sandwiched in between; pin and tack (baste).

6 Mark a gap on one long edge by placing pins approximately 6in (15cm) apart in the centre of the bottom edge. Machine stitch all round with a $5/16$in (8mm) seam allowance, leaving the gap between the pins unstitched.

7 Turn the draught excluder right side out and stuff firmly.

8 On the opening, turn the seam allowance to the inside. Bring the folded edges together and pin, then slipstitch together (see page 15).

9 Stitch the buttons in place for the eyes. Using a long needle, take it right through the head, sewing both buttons in place at the same time.

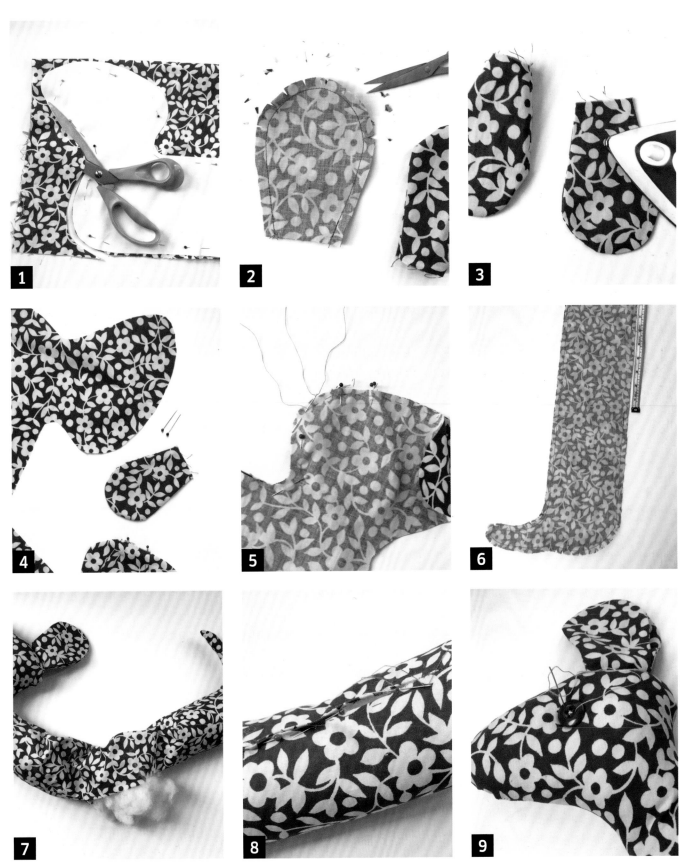

OWL MOBILE

The collective noun for a number of owls is a 'parliament'. This little collection, suspended from a twig, makes good use of a mixed bundle of vintage 1970s-style fabrics in a palette of browns, greens and oranges, which was typical of the era.

Find the templates on pages 148–149

You will need

Pieces of printed cotton fabric (see note)

Pieces of felt (see note)

Six-stranded embroidery thread (floss) in colours to co-ordinate with your fabrics; I used DMC 783 (mustard), 831 (brown) and 921 (burnt orange)

Polyester toy stuffing

2¾yd (2.5m) length of ribbon, ¼in (6mm) wide

Twig or branch, approximately 22in (55cm) long

Chalk pencil or fabric marker

Card or plastic for making patterns

Pins

Dressmaking scissors

General-purpose scissors

Sewing machine

Sewing needle

Embroidery needle

Tweezers (optional)

Corner and edge shaper or similar tool, such as a knitting needle

Thread for tacking (basting)

Thread to match fabric

Iron and ironing board

NOTE: For each owl, you will need a piece of fabric at least 12 x 8in (30 x 20cm), for the back and front, and a contrasting piece at least 8in (20cm) square for the wings. Raid your scrap bag – or shop online for a bundle of vintage patchwork pieces. For the appliqué, you will need felt pieces of the following dimensions and colours: 8 x 3in (20 x 8cm) cream, 6 x 2in (15 x 5cm) orange and 4 x 2in (10 x 5cm) brown (or your choice of colours).

Finished size:
Each owl is approximately 6in (15cm) high and 10¼in (26cm) wide with its wings outstretched

1 Make patterns from card or plastic, using the templates from pages 148 and 149. Place them on a double thickness of fabric, draw around the edges, then cut out the fabric pieces along the lines you have drawn. Use one fabric for the front and back, and a contrast fabric for the wings.

Tip

Translucent plastic is a good choice for cutting the templates needed for this project, as you can see the fabric pattern through the plastic, allowing you to focus on a certain area of the design.

2 From felt, cut out 12 circles 1³⁄₈in (33mm) in diameter for the eyes, 12 circles ½in (12mm) in diameter for the eye centres, and six small triangles for the beaks. Position a pair of eyes 1³⁄₈in (33mm) from the top of the head. Pin the eye centres on the eyes and the beak in between.

3 Thread an embroidery needle with two strands of embroidery thread (floss) and attach the features by stitching all round the edges with blanket stitch (see page 16).

4 Cut three 13½in (34cm) and three 6¼in (16cm) lengths of ribbon. Attach one end of each one to the owls, pinning and tacking (basting) it to the centre top of the head.

5 Place the pairs of wings right sides together and machine stitch with a ⁵⁄₁₆in (8mm) seam allowance, leaving the straight edge open. Clip the corners and snip the curves (see page 21).

6 Turn each wing right side out. This is especially fiddly: you may find a pair of tweezers useful for this task.

7 Use a corner and edge shaper or similar tool to push out the corner of each wing.

8 Lightly stuff each wing with polyester filling. Once again, you might find tweezers useful to complete this.

9 Take a pair of wings and position them on either side of the owl front. Pin and tack in place. Repeat for each of the owls.

10 Match the front and back of each owl. Pin together, tack, then stitch all around with a ⁵⁄₁₆in (8mm) seam allowance, leaving a gap of about 2½in (6cm) in the lower edge for turning. Pull the end of the ribbon through this gap before stitching, to make sure it doesn't get caught in the seam.

11 Turn each owl right side out and stuff with polyester filling. On the opening, turn the seam allowance to the inside, pin together and slipstitch (see page 15) the folded edges together to close the gap.

12 To attach the owls to the twig, loop the end of the ribbon over the twig, fold over the end and oversew the side edges of the ribbon together. Tie the ends of the remaining length of ribbon to the ends of the twig, so that you can hang it up.

BOW TIE

If you wore a bow tie in the 1970s, it was likely to be over-sized. This version is on a more normal scale, but made using fabrics that celebrate the decade of fashion excess. It's pre-tied, so there's no need to stress about how to put it on.

You will need
1 fat quarter of printed cotton fabric
Small piece of medium-weight fusible interfacing (see step 1)
Bow tie set (see note)
Chalk pencil or fabric marker
Pins
Dressmaking scissors
General-purpose scissors
Sewing machine
Sewing needle
Thread for tacking (basting)
Thread to match fabric
Iron and ironing board
Non-stick baking parchment
Loop turner (see page 21)

NOTE: To make the tie adjustable, you will need to purchase a bow tie fastening kit. This consists of a hook, a ring and buckle or slider. The tie fastens by looping the hook over the ring. The strap is lengthened or shortened by pulling the strap through the buckle or slider.

Finished size:
The strap on this bow tie is adjustable, to fit most neck sizes

1 Measure and mark out the pieces for the tie: two rectangles measuring 10¼ x 5⅛in (26 x 13cm), for the bow and two rectangles measuring 26⅜ x 1½in (67 x 4cm) for the strap. Cut these out. You will also need to cut two pieces of fusible interfacing measuring 9½ x 2⅝in (24 x 6.5cm).

2 Place one piece of interfacing in the centre of each of the two bow pieces. Place a piece of non-stick baking parchment on top of the interfacing, to protect the base plate of the iron, and press with a hot iron to fuse in place.

3 Fold the two long edges of each piece towards the centre, folding the fabric along the edge of the interfacing on each side. Press.

4 Now take the two ends of each piece and bring them to meet in the centre. Press.

5 Machine stitch down the centre of each folded piece, on either side, to hold the ends in place.

6 Place the two bow pieces together, with the neat sides facing out. Hand stitch down the centre with a small running stitch, through all thicknesses, to join the two together.

7 Wrap the thread round and round the centre, pulling it tightly, to form the bow shape.

8 To make the bow centre, cut a small rectangle measuring 5 x 3½in (12.5 x 9 cm). Fold the piece in half, right sides together, and stitch down the long edge with a ⅜in (1cm) seam allowance. Press the seam open. Turn right side out, position the seam down the centre of one side, and press. Reserve this piece while you make the strap.

9 To make the strap, join the two pieces along one short edge with a ⅜in (1cm) seam allowance. Press the seam open. Fold the strip in half lengthways, with right sides together, and stitch down the length with a ⅜in (1cm) seam allowance. Trim the seam allowance, then turn the strip right side out with the aid of a loop turner (see page 21).

10 Press the strap. Insert one end through the ring on the hook. Double the end back on itself, tucking the raw end under. Pin, then stitch firmly, oversewing the edges together.

11 Thread the other end of the strap through both spaces on the buckle, through the ring, then back through the buckle. Double the end back on itself, tucking the raw end under. Pin, then stitch firmly, oversewing the edges together.

12 Place the bow in the centre of the strap. Wrap the bow centre around the middle of the bow, with the ends overlapping on the other side of the strap. Fold the ends under, to neaten, then stitch them together.

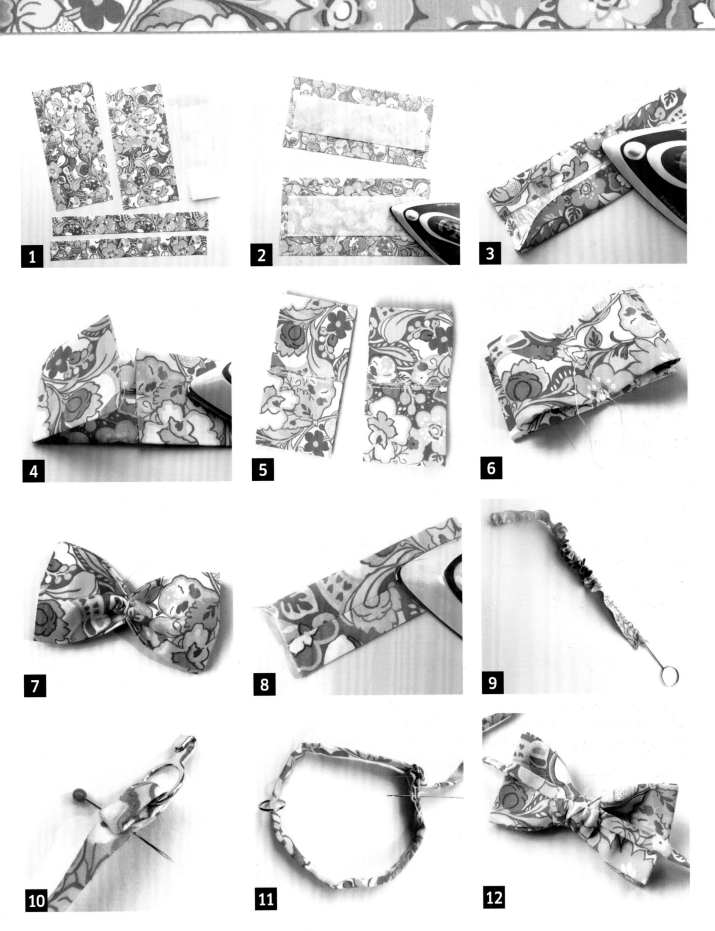

BABY CHANGING MAT

A portable changing mat is an essential item when you are out and about with a baby. It can also be used in the nursery, of course. This one can be folded small enough to fit in a pocket. Lined with towelling, it features a bold Seventies print.

You will need
1 fat quarter each of two different printed cotton fabrics
½yd (50cm) of 55in (142cm) wide towelling (see note)
16in (41cm) of ¼in (7mm) velvet ribbon
16in (41cm) of ½in (12mm) bias binding
2¼yd (2m) of 1in (25mm) bias binding
Large press fastener
Pen or pencil, or tailor's chalk
Pins
Dressmaking scissors
Small scissors
Sewing machine
Sewing needle
Thread to match fabric
Iron and ironing board

NOTE: This project makes the most of a single fat quarter of modern fabric with a Seventies-style print, which is combined with a small piece of vintage fabric salvaged from an old curtain. If you have a larger piece of fabric, you will need a piece measuring about 36 x 16in (90 x 40cm) for the outer part and the inner pocket.

NOTE: Towelling is sold by the yard or metre, so you will need to buy half a yard or metre for this changing mat. Alternatively, you could cut it from a towel.

Finished size:
23 x 15¾in (58 x 40cm)

1 From one printed fat quarter, cut a 15¾in (40cm) square and a rectangle measuring 15¾ x 8in (40 x 20cm). From the other, cut a rectangle measuring 15¾ x 8in (40 x 20cm). From the towelling, cut a piece measuring 23 x 15¾in (58 x 40cm).

2 Join the printed square to the contrasting print rectangle with a ⅜in (1cm) seam allowance. Press the seam open.

3 On the right side, stitch a length of ribbon over the seam line, by hand or machine, for a neat finish.

4 Bind one long edge of the remaining printed piece, using the narrower bias binding and the two-step method described on page 20.

5 To round off each corner, fold the main piece in half, matching the corners, and draw around a small, round object with a diameter of 4½in (11.5cm), such as a saucer, using a chalk pencil. Cut along the line you have drawn. Do the same with the towelling. For the smaller piece, round the corners on the unbound edge only.

6 Place the main piece wrong side up on the work surface. Place the towelling on top, and the piece with the bound edge right side up on top of the towelling, matching the edges and corners. Pin together.

7 Machine stitch all round, ¼in (6mm) from the edge, to join all layers. Trim the edges, if necessary.

8 Bind the changing mat all around, using the wider bias binding. Start at one end of the velvet ribbon. Open out one long edge of the binding and line up the edge with the edge of the fabric. Stitch along the fold by hand or by machine.

9 Flip the mat over, fold the binding over the edge, and slipstitch (see page 15) the folded edge of the binding in place.

10 Sew one half of the press fastener securely to the inside, halfway along the binding on the lower edge. Sew the other half of the fastener to the outside, 5in (12cm) from the top edge and halfway across the width of the mat.

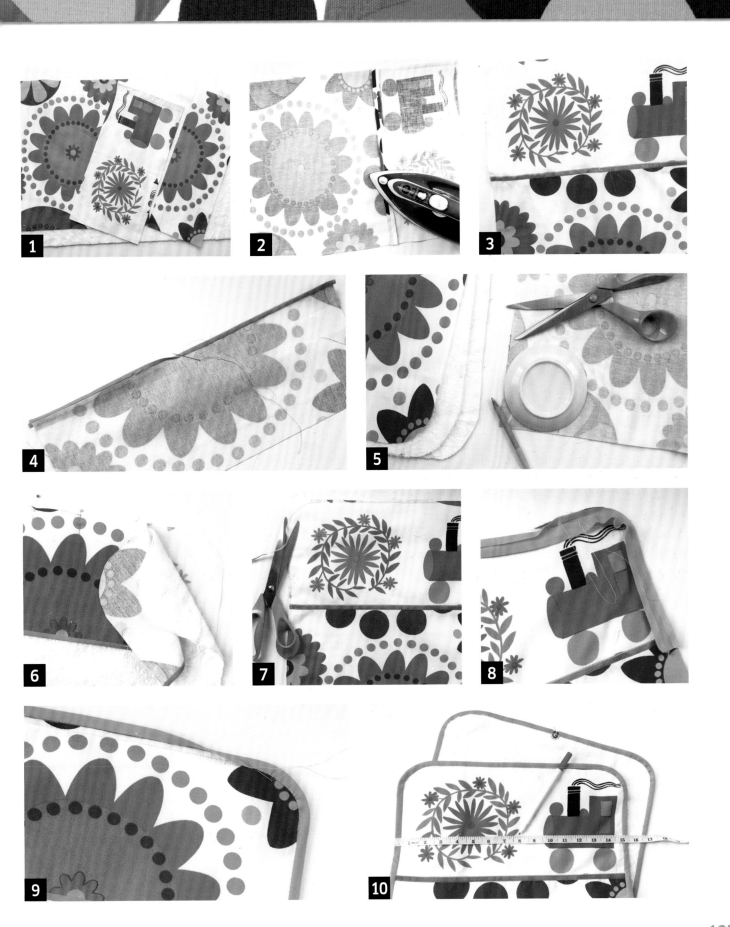

SHOPPING BAG

Plastic carrier bags were first introduced in the 1960s, but after many decades shoppers are now seeking alternatives. Taking a bag with you when you go shopping makes sense, so here's one with a 1970s vibe to fold up and put in your purse or pocket.

You will need
1 fat quarter of printed cotton fabric
1 fat quarter of plain cotton fabric, for lining
43½in (1.1m) length of 1in (25mm) cotton herringbone tape
Chalk pencil or fabric marker
Pins
Dressmaking scissors
General-purpose scissors
Sewing machine
Sewing needle
Thread for tacking (basting)
Thread to match fabric
Iron and ironing board

Finished size is roughly:
10½in (26.5cm) wide and
13in (33cm) long, not including
the handles

1 Trim the printed fat quarter so that it measures 21¾ x 17¾in (55 x 45cm). From this piece cut two strips 2in (5cm) wide, for the handles. For the lining, cut a piece of plain cotton measuring 21¾ x 13¾in (55 x 35cm)

2 Fold the main piece of printed fabric in half lengthways, right sides together, and stitch the side seam with a ³⁄₈in (1cm) seam allowance. Place the seam in the centre of one side and press it open. Do the same with the lining.

3 Stitch across one short edge with a ³⁄₈in (1cm) seam allowance. Do the same with the lining. Clip the corners (see page 21). Turn the main bag right side out. On the raw edge of both bag and lining, turn ³⁄₈in (1cm) to the wrong side and press. Slip the lining inside the bag, wrong sides together.

4 Now take the two pieces for the handles and fold ³⁄₈in (1cm) to the wrong side along each long edge. Press.

5 Cut the cotton herringbone tape into two equal lengths. Place one down the centre of each handle, covering the raw edges. Machine stitch in place down both sides of the tape.

6 Lining up the seams, pin the top edge of the bag and lining together; insert the ends of the two handles between the two layers as you do so.

7 Topstitch (see page 19) through all layers, close to the top edge, and again about ¹⁄₈–¹⁄₄in (3–5mm) below this line.

Tip

Using cotton herringbone tape – available from all good haberdashers – to reinforce the fabric handles makes this bag sturdy and practical.

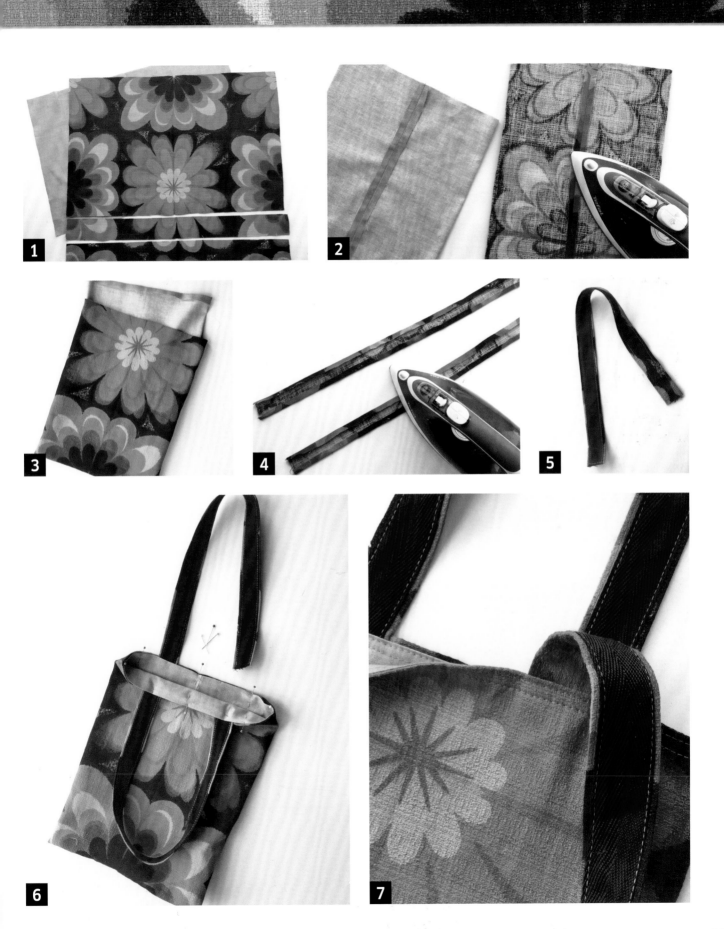

TEMPLATES

Templates shown at actual size can be traced and cut out, or photocopied.

For templates reduced in size, enlarge them on an A3 photocopier to the percentage stated.

TRAY CLOTH

Page 32
Copy at 176%

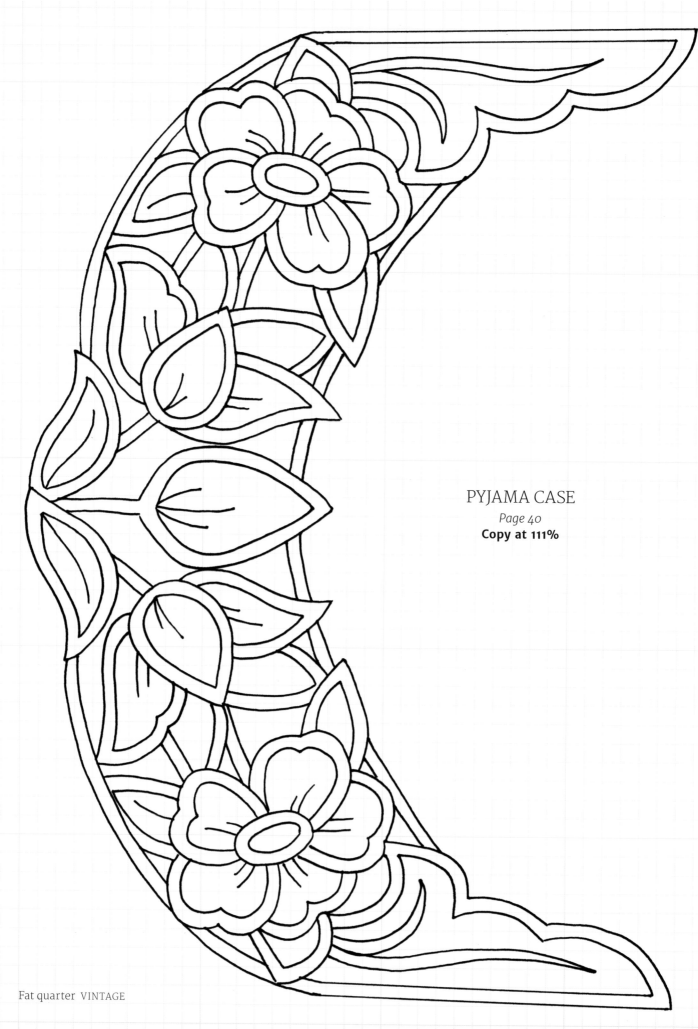

PYJAMA CASE
Page 40
Copy at 111%

SEWING MACHINE COVER
Page 50
Copy at 125%
side

COAT HANGER COVER

Page 54
Copy at 111%

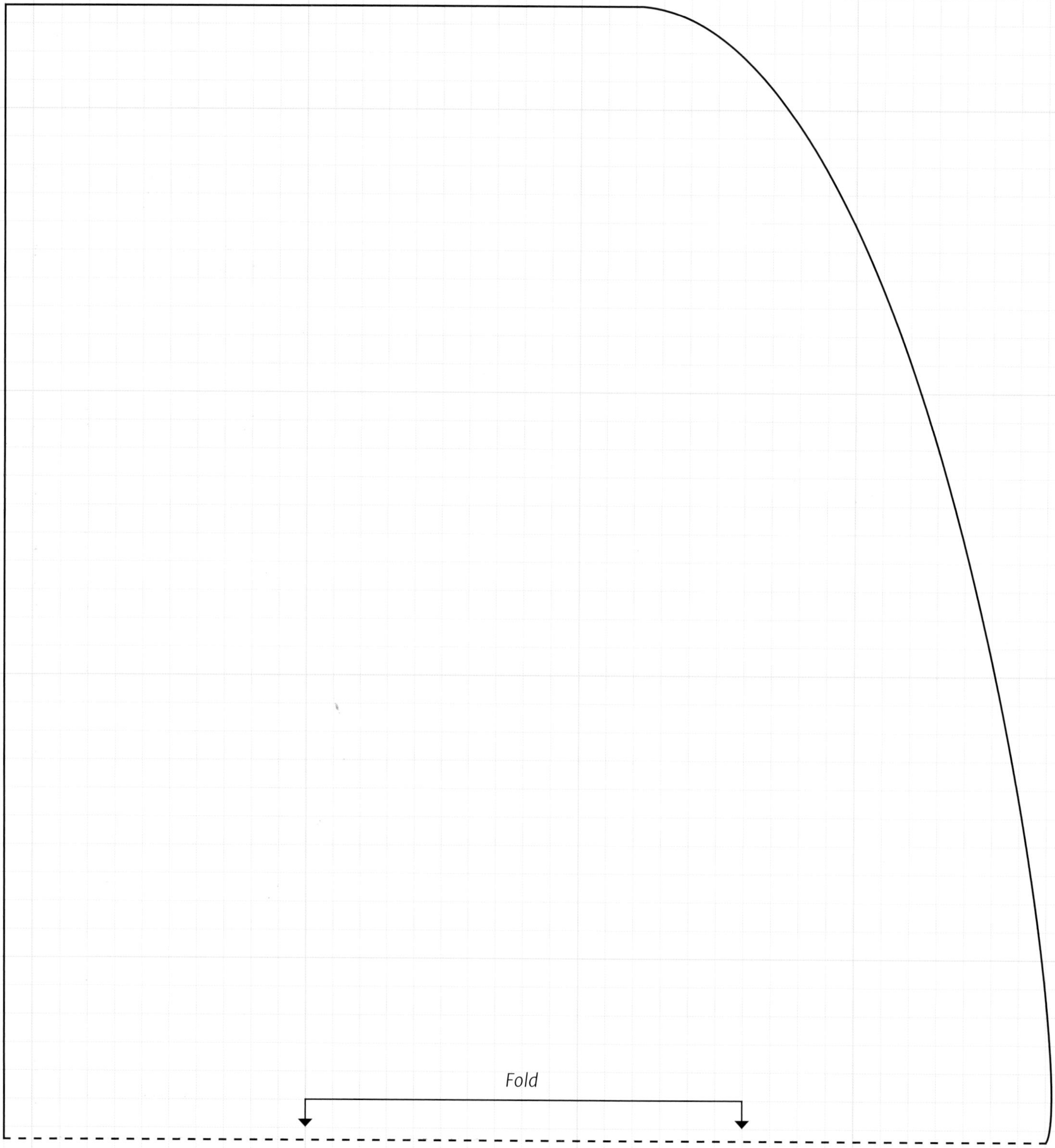

Fold

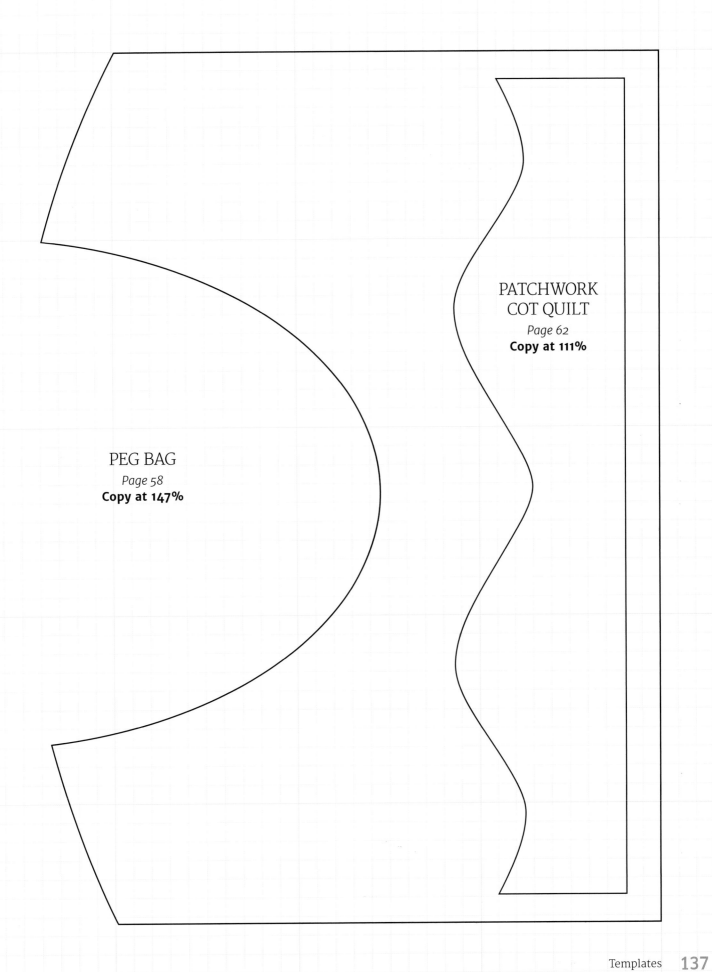

PATCHWORK
COT QUILT
Page 62
Copy at 111%

PEG BAG
Page 58
Copy at 147%

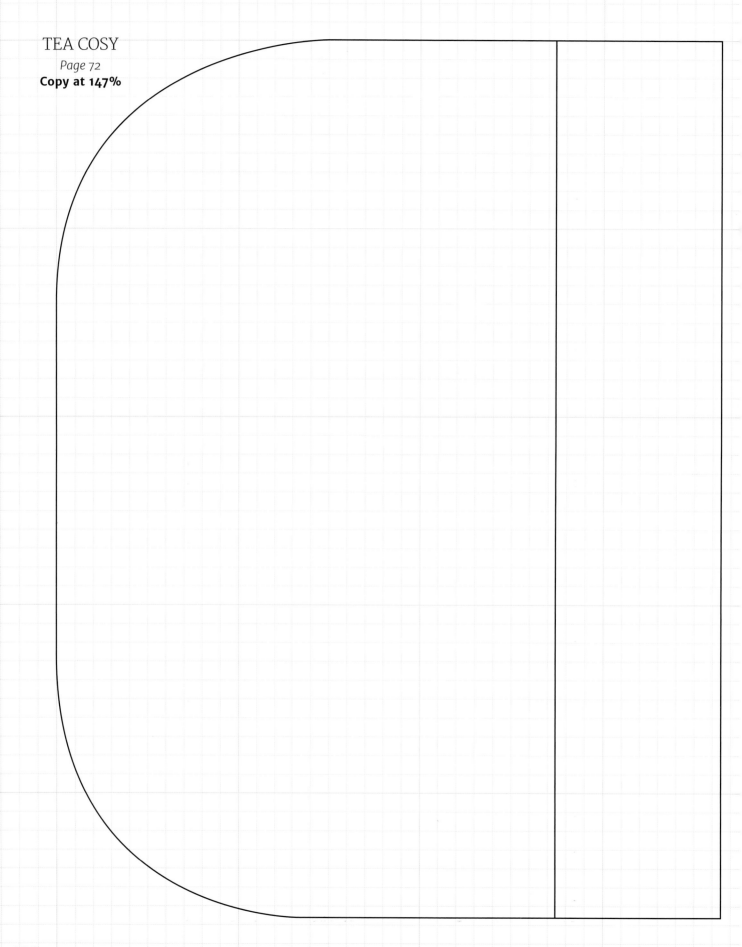

TEA COSY
Page 72
Copy at 147%

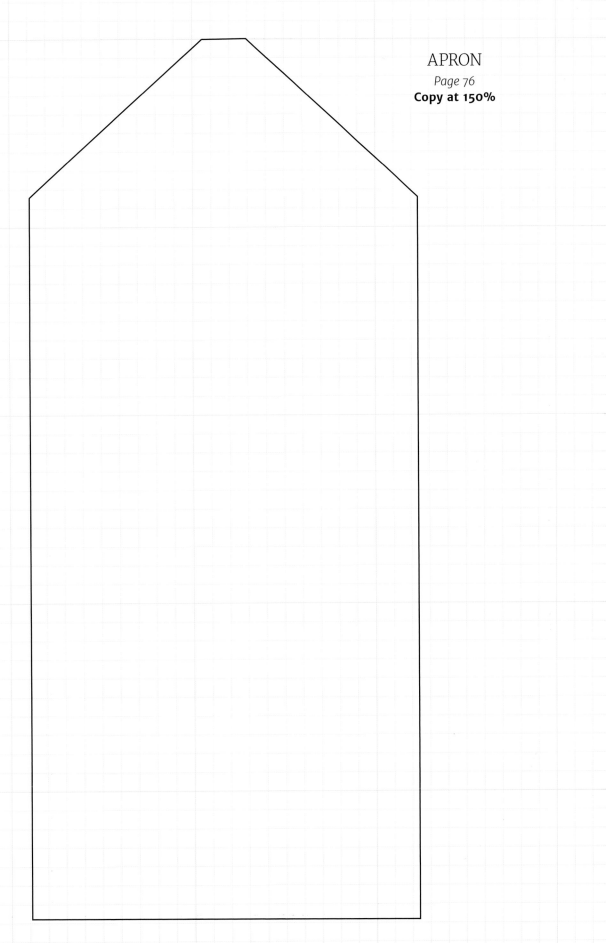

APRON
Page 76
Copy at 150%

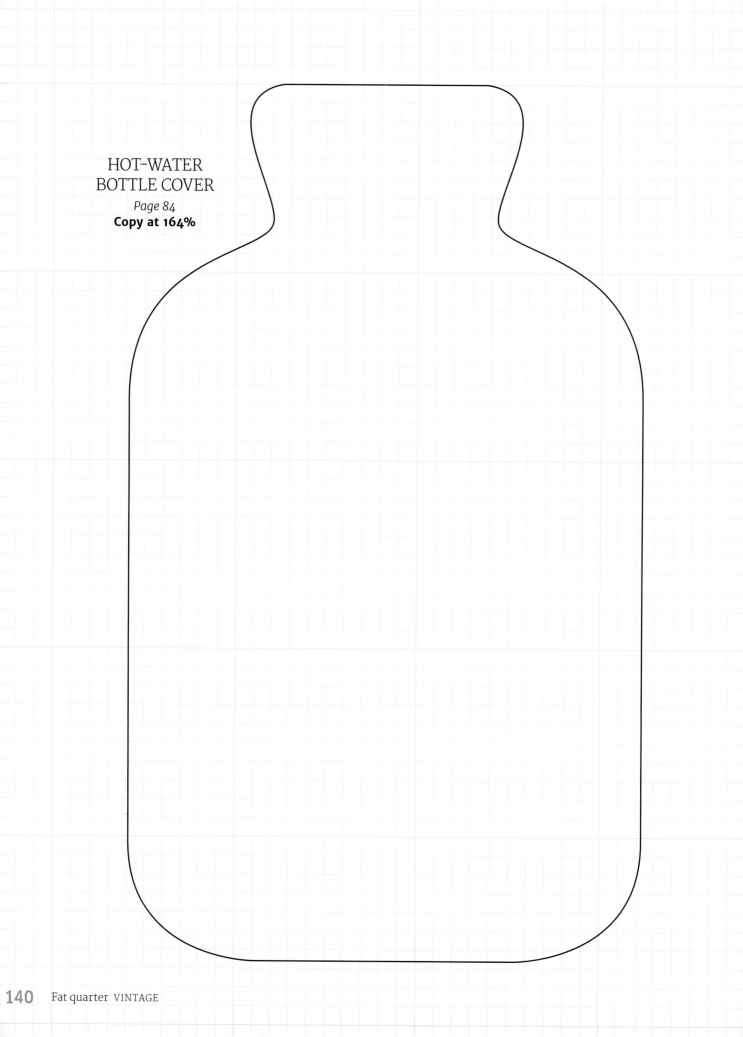

HOT–WATER
BOTTLE COVER
Page 84
Copy at 164%

APPLIQUÉ CUSHION
Page 90
Copy at 100%

APPLIQUÉ CUSHION

Page 90
Copy at 100%

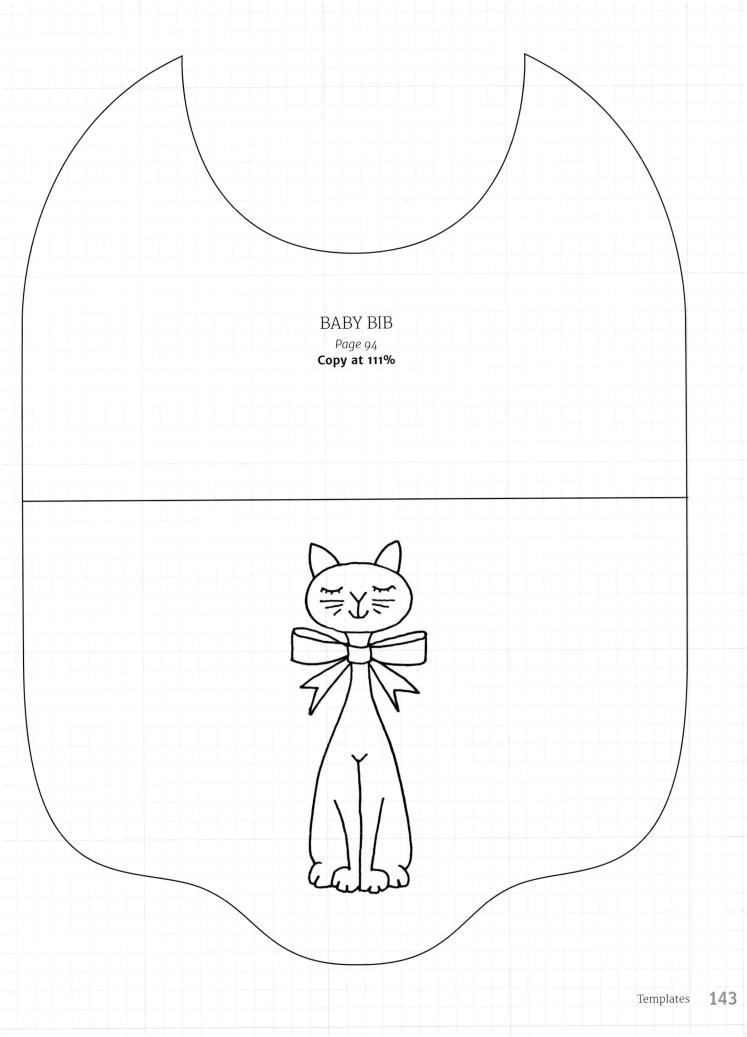

BABY BIB

Page 94
Copy at 111%

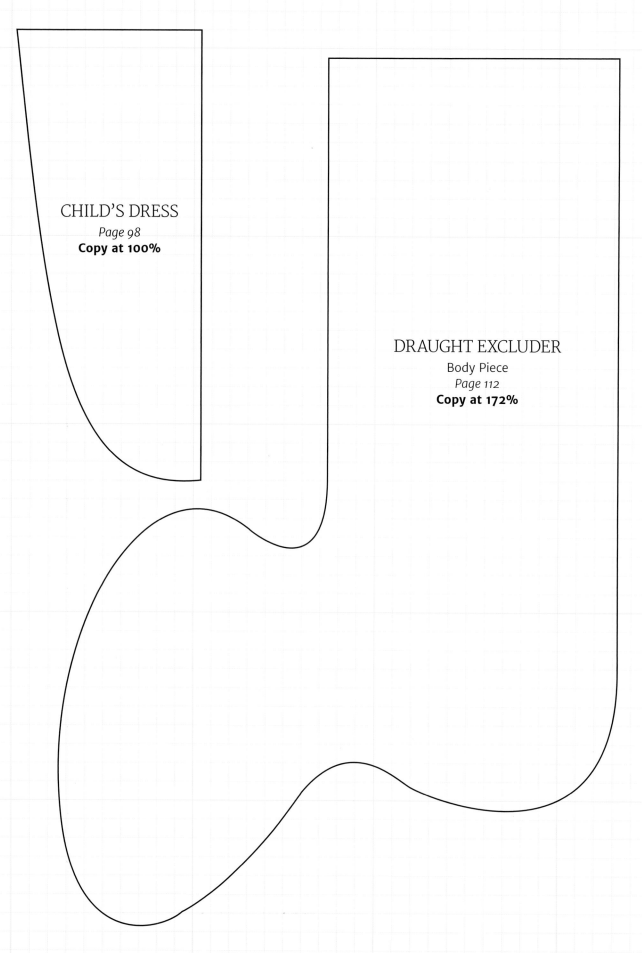

CHILD'S DRESS
Page 98
Copy at 100%

DRAUGHT EXCLUDER
Body Piece
Page 112
Copy at 172%

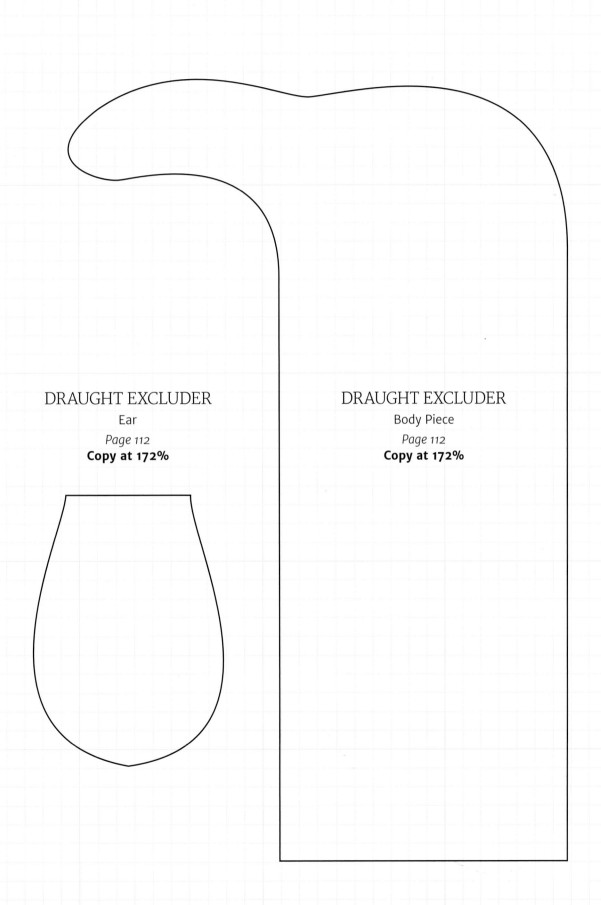

DRAUGHT EXCLUDER

Ear

Page 112

Copy at 172%

DRAUGHT EXCLUDER

Body Piece

Page 112

Copy at 172%

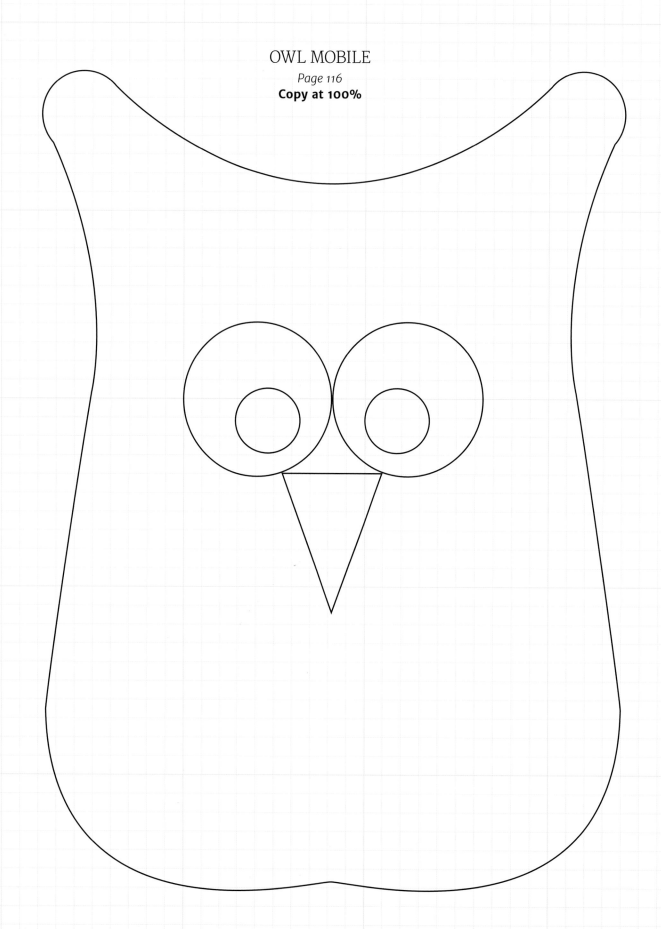

OWL MOBILE

Page 116

Copy at 100%

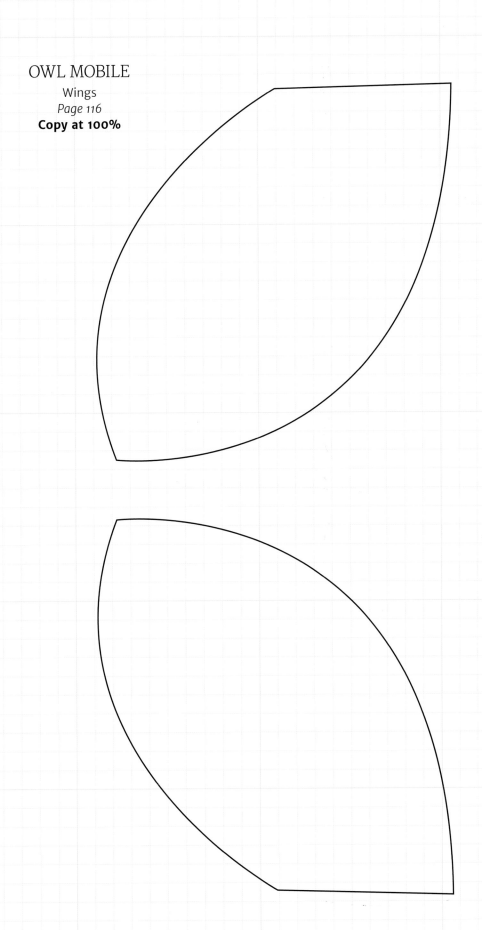

OWL MOBILE
Wings
Page 116
Copy at 100%

RESOURCES

Original vintage fabrics
donnaflowervintage.com
rickrack.com
vintagefabrics.com.au

Reproduction fabrics
fabric.com
spoonflower.com

Vintage buttons
thebuttonbower.com
vintagebuttons.net

Cotton fabrics, fat quarters
craftcotton.com
fabricland.co.uk

Measuring and marking tools
prym.com

Fusible interfacing and fleece
empressmills.co.uk
plushaddict.co.uk

General haberdashery
sewandso.co.uk
sewing-online.com

Embroidery threads, quilter's square
cottonpatch.co.uk
sewessential.co.uk

Sewing machines and accessories
jaycotts.co.uk
sewingmachines.co.uk

ACKNOWLEDGEMENTS

Many thanks to Jonathan Bailey for commissioning me to write this book, to Dominique Page for being such a supportive editor, and to Gilda Pacitti and her team for designing the book. The publisher and I would also like to thank: Anna and William Stevens, Arthur, Ivy and Nancy Motley for modelling; Anna Stevens for providing the location for the shoot; and Wayne Blades for the photography styling.

INDEX

To order a book, or to request
a catalogue, contact:

GMC Publications Ltd
Castle Place, 166 High Street,
Lewes, East Sussex,
BN7 1XU
United Kingdom
Tel: +44 (0)1273 488005
www.gmcbooks.com